Tough Customers

Counseling Unwilling Clients

Edited by George A. Harris, Ph.D.

Copyright 1991 by the American Correctional Association.
All rights reserved.

Patricia L. Poupore, Director of Communications and Publications
Elizabeth Watts, Publications Managing Editor
Becky E. Hagenston, Editorial Assistant
Ralph Butler, Cover Design

The reproduction, distribution, or inclusion in other publications of materials in this book is prohibited without prior written permission from the American Correctional Association.

ISBN 0-929310-57-8

Printed in the U. S. A. by Goodway Graphics, Springfield, Va.

This publication may be ordered from:
American Correctional Association
8025 Laurel Lakes Court
Laurel, Md. 20707-5075
1-800-825-BOOK

Table of Contents

Foreword
    Anthony P. Travisono iv

Introduction
    George A. Harris, Ph.D. v

Dealing With Difficult Clients
    George A. Harris, Ph.D. 1

Some Practical Methods of Treating the Mandated Client
    Jerry Larke 12

Identifying and Confronting Resistance in Lifestyle Criminal Offenders
    Glenn D. Walters 25

"Rehabilitating" White Collar Criminals
    George A. Harris, Ph.D. 43

Working With the Resistant Cocaine Abuser
    Harry M. Brown, Ph.D. 55

Counseling the Resistant Chemically Dependent Adolescent
    Gregg J. Stockey, M. S., and Daun D. Blain, M. S. 65

Developing a Therapeutic Alliance in the Hospital Treatment of Disturbed Adolescents
    Flynn O'Malley, Ph.D. 73

Intervention Strategies for Sexual Abuse
    Robert Rencken 86

Perpetrators of Domestic Violence: An Overview of Counseling the Court-mandated Client
    Anne L. Ganley 113

Influencing Reluctant Elderly Clients to Participate in Mental Health Counseling
    Floyd F. Robison, Marlowe H. Smaby,
    Gary L. Donovan 134

Foreword

Many therapists don't believe in wasting their time on people who are reluctant to make substantial changes in their lives. This view may govern the world of voluntary counseling, but it doesn't apply to clients who only show up because the court or some other authority orders it.

Counseling difficult clients is not easy and never will be. Thousands of mental health professionals and counselors go to work each day wondering, "Why bother?" How can clients be helped if they won't participate in their own treatment?

In this book of readings, George Harris has collected articles that explore specific problems faced by counselors who work with involuntary clients. These articles are invaluable not only to the corrections professional who must counsel lifestyle criminals, cocaine abusers, and sex offenders, but also to any counselor faced with the daunting task of treating difficult clients. The insights and practical techniques offered here can be used by counselors in schools, hospitals, and mental health clinics.

Breaking through a tough customer's resistance is the first step in working towards a productive relationship with the counselor, which is vital to the success of any treatment program. This book should be required reading for all active counselors, therapists, and students of counseling techniques.

Anthony P. Travisono
Executive Director
American Correctional Association

Introduction

After completing *Counseling the Involuntary and Resistant Client* (Harris and Watkins 1987), I began offering workshops to counselors around the country on the topic. Many of the workshop participants were counselors without graduate training in counseling and therapy who, because of their own life experiences, had begun to work in drug and alcohol treatment programs and other agencies treating clients with extremely difficult problems. These counselors often work from their intuition and are suspicious of impractical academic theory. Yet it is important to develop a logical rationale for conducting counseling. Otherwise, we might as well rely on sorcery and incantations, the effectiveness of which is assumed rather than scientifically measured, understood, and criticized.

It seemed that the involuntary client book and workshops were meeting a need and that the decision to emphasize practical solutions had been good. This was so despite the objections of an early academic reviewer of the book, who said that it was unethical because it recommended techniques for working with clients who didn't want to be counseled. I wondered where this reviewer had been hiding out for the last two decades. Meloy et al.'s manual, *Clinical Guidelines for Involuntary Outpatient Treatment* (1990), is the only other work I am aware of that specifically addresses the issue of involuntary clients. I highly recommend it. There are a number of good books on treating sex offenders, criminals, substance abusers, and other groups, and of course there are many correctional psychology texts, but it seems strange that there is so little written focusing on the issue of involuntariness in counseling.

Even well-trained therapists needed some review of basic counseling concepts for working with difficult clients. Therapists with graduate degrees seemed to have the same problems working with difficult clients as lesser-trained counselors, notably a tendency to give up too easily by saying that the client could return when he or she was ready to work.

At workshops, counselors working with special populations posed a number of unique questions. Counselors working with sex offenders had issues somewhat different from counselors working with addiction problems. Counselors working with criminal populations had questions different from counselors working with adolescents. Therapists working in hospitals had unique concerns about their difficult patients.

It seemed that the general principles of working with involuntary and resistant clients remained common but that some discussion of how to work with specific problems would be helpful. The questions posed to me at workshops created the concept for the present book of readings, whose purpose is to explore issues of involuntary and resistant clients with special populations in differing settings. Included are articles on sex offenders, hospitalized adolescents, chemically dependent adolescents, cocaine abusers, and white collar offenders. There is also an interesting article on working with the reluctant elderly that demonstrates how involuntariness affects noncorrectional clients, too.

It would be impossible to include in any book an article on every identifiable problem that forces clients into treatment. The variety is enormous. Articles were selected and solicited on enough subjects to provide a good variety of special viewpoints. The authors' recommendations may at times appear inconsistent with each other, but there is more agreement than disagreement, because involuntary clients have much in common.

I gradually have come to think of involuntary clients as falling into three broad categories. The first is the thought-disordered client. As Meloy et al. (1990) point out, persons with thought disorders (schizophrenia and other psychoses) are frequently involuntarily committed for treatment, and it is important to understand the need first for control of the thought disorder through medication. Then other axis II personality disorders may become apparent and call for treatment. For example, a person with a schizophrenic disorder may also have an underlying antisocial personality disorder. The treatment of such clients requires psychiatric leadership because of the need for medication, though psychological and social treatment is needed to help patients understand and comply with directions for taking medication and to deal with the social effects of a psychotic illness. For example, it is important with such clients to understand how to control the stressful effects of social interaction on them.

The second broad category of involuntary and resistant clients is offender populations. Though there was some discussion of criminal thinking in *Counseling the Involuntary and Resistant Client*, it seemed important to provide in the present book of readings a description of "the criminal personality" and criminal thinking. Yochelson and Samenow's work on this subject is a primary reference, and Glenn Walters's chapter herein provides an excellent synthesis of and addition to that work. Sex offenders and many substance abusers also fall under the category of "criminal offenders," though as Harry Brown's article on cocaine abusers points out, working with cocaine-abusing clients poses problems not found among even other drug users.

The third broad category of involuntary and resistant clients is difficult to label. I call them the PILs: people with Problems In Living. They are not thought-disordered in the sense of having a psychotic illness, nor do they really have criminal personalities, though like all of us they may display irresponsible thinking and behavior at times. They may have problems with authority figures. They may be angry and rebellious or sad and suicidal. To use an old term, they may be neurotic. Many juveniles in correctional treatment have no psychiatric disorder and as the articles by O'Malley and Stockey and Blain illustrate, juveniles need to be examined with respect to developmental issues.

The PILs major resistance is "righteous resistance." They resist making changes that would be in their best interest because they simply don't want someone else telling them what to do or because the change demanded is inconsistent with their self-concept in some way. Their motto is "I'd rather fight than switch." An effective method of dealing with this resistance is to help people identify their "righteous" feelings and talk about them before trying to get them to talk about the problem that was the identified reason for referral. For example, before talking with clients about a drug problem, I first try to get them to talk about their feelings about being coerced into treatment. Or I try to help them talk about the way that using drugs fits into their images of themselves. (Do they see themselves as hip? independent? risk taking? defiant? tough?) Paradoxically, when counselors empathize with the purpose of the client's behavior, the client feels more free to see the disadvantages of the behavior.

A problem that was briefly addressed in *Counseling the Involuntary and Resistant Client* has seemed even more important in the years since publication: the problem of transference and counter-transference issues. Sometimes clients resist the counselor because the therapist comes to represent authority. As Meloy et al. (1990) point out, the involuntary client may perceive the counseling relationship as a re-creation of his or her first involuntary relationship, the relationship between parent and child. Such a transference is bound to be powerful, as is the counter-transference reaction of the counselor who reacts to the client's rebellion. In this instance, the client's resistance is exacerbated by the therapists' counter-transference.

Unfortunately, counselors often create much of the client's resistance. This happens with clumsy, offensive approaches that would annoy just about anyone, much less the client who has been forced into treatment. The resistance created by therapist blundering could be called "iatrogenic" resistance, or doctor-induced resistance. Unfortunately, a high percentage of the resistance problems found is caused by the therapist's unwillingness or inability to use the client's language, define problems from the client's perspective, and talk about feelings related to being coerced before diving into the "official" reason for the referral. Many therapists begin confronting clients before the clients are ready to be confronted and before any sort of therapeutic alliance has been established.

Some of this impatience to confront may stem from therapeutic nihilism—the skepticism that therapy can work—especially with correctional clients. We have seen more than a decade of criticism of correctional rehabilitation, and it is unfortunate when therapists allow such criticism to become a self-fulfilling prophecy.

The most common complaint I get from participants in my workshops is this: "I don't have time to do all that relationship building. We get these clients for a month and that's it." I respond that nobody expects a neurosurgeon to operate in thirty minutes. Counseling takes some time, and if that time is not provided, it doesn't help to crack open the skull with a sledgehammer to get to the tumor. The patient might not survive. Counselors should not apologize for being unable to get results when given inadequate time and resources to do the job. Counselors should not try to do the impossible task of being one-minute brain surgeons.

Therapists seldom seem to ask their clients how they define their problems, how they believe their problems are caused, and what they believe will help. These seem like such simple things to do, and these questions elicit so much information. But perhaps especially with involuntary clients therapists fall into the role of the agent of coercion. By thinking through the issues of working with involuntary and resistant clients with various problems, perhaps we can learn to listen better.

George A. Harris, Ph.D.

References

Harris, G., and D. Watkins. 1987. *Counseling the involuntary and resistant client*. Laurel, Md.: American Correctional Association.

Meloy, R., A. Haroun, and E. Schiller. 1990. *Clinical guidelines for involuntary outpatient treatment*. Sarasota, Fla.: Professional Resource Exchange.

Dealing With Difficult Clients

George A. Harris, Ph.D.

Every counselor encounters clients who are difficult, though what one counselor finds difficult, another may not. The counseling literature is replete with discussion of "resistance," but as Anderson and Stewart (1983) state, resistance is often defined as whatever clients do that counselors don't want them to do.

Despite disagreements in defining difficult clients and resistance, it is possible to identify some common causes of treatment problems. These causes can be observed by looking at resistance to change, to the counselor, and to counseling itself. Other factors are counselors' reactions to clients that may impede treatment and client accessibility to treatment.

Resistance to Change

Most theories of counseling have an explanation of resistance to change. Behaviorists identify the cause of resistance as inadequate reinforcement; family therapists see resistance as a function of the system's efforts to maintain homeostasis and keep the status quo; rational-emotive therapists view resistance as caused by irrational beliefs; psychodynamic theories hold that the unconscious prevents awareness of material that would cause psychic distress.

It is important not to view all resistance as bad. Ellis (1985) points out that clients may resist therapists' suggestions because the suggestions are just wrong. Ansbacher (1981) argues that resistance is a necessary result of stability and integrity of personality. After all, if a person never resisted change, he or she would never settle on a career, a spouse, or even an opinion. The counselor's job is not to remove resistance to change, but only those resistances that are dysfunctional for the client.

Resistance to the Counselor

Many theories of psychotherapy consider transference to be an issue to be dealt with in counseling. During the course of counseling, the client may have a reaction to the counselor that seems to based on imagined truths about the relationship that has developed. The client confuses the counselor with someone else, often a parent or authority figure, sometimes a sibling, or occasionally just someone who looks like the counselor. Understanding these reactions is an important tool for helping the client learn to deal with people objectively rather than as mirages and reminders of past unrelated encounters. Transference issues are especially important when working with clients who have been coerced into counseling. Such clients come from correctional, substance abuse, and many other rehabilitation programs. Meloy et al. (1990) remark that the involuntary client has special transference issues because the therapeutic encounter mirrors the early parent/child relationship, which was biologically an involuntary one for the client. Most therapists overlook or minimize the problem of involuntariness in counseling (Harris and Watkins 1987). In their zeal to begin talking about the client's "problem," counselors don't spend enough time dealing with the resistance that is created by the mere fact that counseling was not the client's choice. The result is that the client's view of the counselor as an agent of coercion is never challenged.

Resistance to Counseling

Most counseling theories assume that the counseling relationship is voluntary and that treatment cannot be initiated ethically until permission to counsel is granted (Shertzer and Stone 1974). The reality is that thousands of clients every day are counseled without consent in prisons, drug programs, and even in private practices. Thus, it is useful to think about resistance to counseling as separate from resistance to change and the counselor.

Many behavior problems and psychological disorders, such as substance abuse, are accompanied by intense denial, and these clients do not seek treatment until they are forced. Even in marriage counseling, it is typical for one spouse to be eager for counseling while the other resists. The counselor may wish to differentiate "counseling" from "preparing the client for counseling," as a way out of an ethical quagmire. In a sense, the client needs to be sold on the value of counseling. The client needs to be convinced that counseling can help in some way. It is not unethical to help clients discuss their feelings, objections, and concerns about being coerced into treatment. Such discussion is the beginning of the formation of a therapeutic relationship, though the specific reason why the client was referred may hardly be mentioned. After thoroughly exploring the issues related to participation in counseling, either counselor or client may elect not to continue.

Most theories of counseling have an explanation of resistance to change and resistance to the counselor, some in more detail than others. However, few theories directly address or give recommendations for resolving the resistance to counseling that many clients show. So it may be helpful to expand our understanding of why clients object to counseling.

There are many practical reasons why clients resist counseling—expense and inconvenience, for example. There are other reasons that are related to the resistance for change—for example, the client fears change, which is what counseling represents. There are three primary reasons why clients resist entering treatment:

- mistrust or cynicism about the value of talk in solving problems
- psychological reaction to a perceived loss of freedom
- the client's belief that the problem is external to self and therefore cannot be solved by personal initiative

Mistrust of counseling and counselors is understandable considering how often people feel that they have been deceived by promises from authority in their lives. This feeling of having been misled leads to cynicism and pessimism and therefore reluctance to participate in counseling. Many clients mistrust not only counseling but also themselves and their own capacity to change. They've told themselves before they would change, and didn't, and don't understand how counseling could help. Thus, not only people but language itself is doubted. Counseling is dismissed as only talk, and "talk is cheap."

The second reason why clients resist counseling is that they object to any kind of coercion and restriction of freedom (Dowd and Seibel 1990). It is crucial that counseling be portrayed as an opportunity to increase freedom by pointing out that the process is designed not to restrict but to increase alternatives. This may be difficult for clients to see in the abstract, but counselors can try to make the point. Most important, counselors can try to give clients as many choices as possible in appointment times, topics to discuss, and even seating arrangements. Such attention to choices demonstrates rather than merely describes the nonrestrictive nature of the process.

The final major cause of resistance to counseling is the

client's belief that his or her problems are external to self. After all, if the problems are the fault of parents, schools, spouses, or society in general, why would clients think anything they could change would make a difference? Clients often say, "You've got the wrong person in here. You should fix ____."

Of course it is often difficult to persuade people that they are responsible for their own dilemma. Most counseling theories not only assume that a voluntary relationship exists between counselor and client but also that the client perceives personal responsibility for the problem. Such personal responsibility would be accompanied by anxiety or guilt, while externalizing responsibility is accompanied by anger or blame.

The latter are emotions less likely to evoke sympathy in counselors and more likely to elicit rejection and distancing from the client. This clearly makes treatment more difficult.

Counselor Response to Difficult Clients

When clients react negatively, the counselor's response will, of course, affect the progress of treatment. There are several frequent and understandable counselor responses or countertransference reactions.

Clients who view counselors as authority or parental figures and act rebelliously will sometimes elicit authoritarian, critical, parental behavior from counselors. It is often hard not to have punishing or rejecting feelings toward clients who act out their dislike of authority, even when one consciously knows why such behavior is happening. Many clients devalue and disparage counselors' efforts to be helpful, and this may cause counselors to feel rage and rejection (Meloy et al. 1990).

When clients are violent or intimidating, many counselors understandably feel threatened and afraid, feelings that both inhibit the desire to help and/or confront and arouse basic defenses. Those defenses typically manifest in fight or flight behavior, but some counselors may feel frozen, numb, or paralyzed in the face of physical threat.

Just as clients often harbor mistrust of words, and therefore counseling, as a result of prior broken promises in life, so too may counselors. Counselors who are deceived or misled by resistant clients may experience an arousal of a range of feelings from anger to disgust that recreate feelings from their own earlier life experiences (Meloy et al. 1990). When counselors work frequently with clients who lie or deceive, they may develop cynical attitudes that are apparent to all clients and sabotage the counseling process. This becomes self-fulfilling prophecy as counselors anticipate being deceived, and not wanting to appear gullible, they approach all clients as potential liars. Clients in turn oblige the expectation because they are predisposed not to believe in the possibility of an accepting and honest relationship. And so it goes. The end result of this cycle is therapeutic nihilism, a counselor's cynical doubt that counseling can be effective with certain groups of people (Meloy et al. 1990).

Some counselors doubt that anyone will honestly participate in a change process. Often counselors believe everyone will. Therapists may overrate the development of the treatment alliance and progress with clients who in reality are going nowhere (Meloy et al. 1990). While it is difficult to be critical of anyone who is optimistic, the term *hopeless optimist* does suggest that optimism should be tempered with realism if for no other reason than that valuable resources can be wasted on people who are not being helped.

Counselors often misunderstand clients by assuming that together they share experiences, feelings, and values (Meloy et al. 1990). This is an especially important problem when working with antisocial clients, who may deliberately lead the counselor into giving rosy assessments of therapeutic progress. Such assessments may be advantageous to clients who are trying to achieve early release from treatment. Therapists need to be particularly alert to clients who display guilt and remorse when none exist. It is hard for many therapists to comprehend that some clients do not truly experience normal guilt.

It is probably impossible for counselors not to be either a little too pessimistic or optimistic at the beginning of treatment. We all have our own personalities and world views and cannot be totally objective. Perhaps the most dangerous effect of the counselor's personality on the client is the unconscious encouragement of acting out, rebellion, or misbehavior. Some counselors gain vicarious satisfaction from their clients' sexual encounters or flouting of authority. Clients who are already predisposed to inappropriate behavior are easily encouraged when therapists grin at tales of escapades or encourage accounts of binges or lost weekends. Counselors should seek consultation if their clients seem to get consistently worse rather than better in treatment while the counseling sessions seem to be friendly and productive.

In summary, not all client resistance comes strictly from the client. The counselor's reactions to the client's behavior may exacerbate the problem. Some therapists are cynical toward clients, and their attitudes discourage treatment relationships; sometimes the counselor may unconsciously desire the client to misbehave. This is iatrogenic (doctor-induced) resistance. Therapists' reactions to provocation and intimidation may impede treatment by blocking their desire to help or confront.

Counseling Approaches to the Difficult Client

There is no one counseling theory on which everyone can agree, and the disagreement compounds when the client is difficult. Nevertheless, it is possible to categorize several different general approaches and discuss the pros and cons of each.

Most counselors are familiar with emotive approaches. These are counseling styles aimed at reflecting the client's feelings and cognitions to encourage exploration and self-examination as well as develop the relationship between counselor and client. Therapists from person-centered counselors to psychoanalysts may use active listening techniques to achieve these goals. Weiss (1990) describes recent research on unconscious functioning from a psychodynamic perspective, which sees resistance as the unconscious blocking of interpersonal disclosure until safety is perceived by the person. This research has profound implications for psychotherapy in supporting the concept of accepting, nonjudgemental relationships as important for therapeutic progress.

It is important when working with difficult clients not to focus too quickly on the problem that triggered the referral. Many counselors are eager to begin problem solving and do not give enough time for clients to explore their feelings about having been coerced into treatment. Given the understandable fear that many clients have about being direct and open about their feelings, it becomes all the more important to build relationships and develop trust. As Weiss pointed out, the resistance may be unconscious, but the client may be well aware of the resistance to participate. In either case, when the counselor pushes too rapidly into the reason for referral, important opportunities to establish a cooperative relationship are lost.

A second general category or approach is cognitive therapy. With difficult clients cognitive therapists may elect to challenge the clients' beliefs that inhibit participation in counseling and cooperation with the counselor. For example, some involuntary clients may resist participating in treatment because they believe that they should get to do what they want to do when they want to do it or that they shouldn't have to do what they don't want to do. Rational emotive therapists often attack such statements with logic and evidence. Such confrontation, however, may arouse defensiveness. In advocating forceful persuasion, Ellis (1985) acknowledges that persuasion is called for when the client resists change but that relationship building is essential when the client resists the counselor.

Lyddon (1990) describes two major types of cognitive therapies. One type deals with surface change of irrational thoughts and beliefs; the second type deals with deeper change of personal constructs and patterns of belief. Change of personal constructs is not easily amenable to argumentation and syllogistic reasoning but rather requires reflection and affective expression to facilitate cognitive restructuring. When clients have deep-seated characterological difficulties, it does not seem likely that they will be able to examine their core difficulties without first developing some confidence and trust in a therapeutic ally. This makes relationship building again appear important.

A third general kind of approach for working with difficult clients is the strategic or paradoxical approach. It is beyond the scope of this paper to give a full explanation of any approach, but paradoxical approaches are especially difficult to summarize. Sometimes when clients are defiant, paradoxical interventions can create cognitive binds that impose change. For example, when a client who doesn't trust the counselor is told that such mistrust is understandable, confusion results. The client hears a trustworthy statement from someone he or she didn't expect to trust. The counselor might even direct the client to act cautiously based on the mistrust. A defiant client then becomes "compliant" by following the counselor's directive. These paradoxical directives must be used cautiously. Unfortunately, it is tempting to use them as manipulative gimmicks rather than as well-thought-out strategies for helping the person.

Other paradoxical strategies involve the use of exaggeration to reshape the client's perception. For example, a client who admits to not trusting the counselor might be asked if he or she mistrusts everything about the counselor. Few clients will admit that they believe the counselor is really a spy for the FBI, and some light-hearted teasing about this may help establish that trust and mistrust are on a continuum. It then becomes easier to explore degrees of trust and mistrust and ways to improve the relationship. Of course, if clients do think the counselor is a spy from the FBI, it might be wise to consider a medication review.

Another paradoxical strategy involves examination of positive intent behind negative behavior. Resistance must be seen as a necessary component of stability and integrity in the personality. People do what they do for reasons they think are appropriate or, at least, justified. For example, parents who are harsh with their children may feel that the harshness is justified to teach their children correct behavior. The parents' intent is positive although the effects of the behavior may not be. Counselors who can identify positive intent and acknowledge understanding of it to the client may arouse less defensiveness from the client. This in turn may allow the client to explore the effectiveness of the behavior in achieving the desired goal.

When people feel personally criticized, they defend themselves by attacking their attacker.

Finally, paradoxical strategies acknowledge the great ambivalence that lies behind any significant change. A person with an alcohol problem, for example, has many reasons to quit drinking: health, expense, job security, family relationships, etc. But there are many reasons not to quit as well: loss of drinking companions, facing personal problems when sober and not anaesthetized, and so on. A counselor who simply confronts the client with all the reasons to quit drinking will meet with great resistance because the reasons to continue drinking are still operative. Paradoxically, when the counselor can empathize with the client's ambivalence to change, the client is freer to fully explore both sides of the issue and take responsibility for the decision whatever it may be.

States of Accessibility With Difficult Clients

Clients are sometimes not ready for counseling. When involuntary clients resist the very idea of counseling, the counselor must "sell" the client on the process. Menninger (1958) described all psychotherapy with this sales metaphor and contended that even voluntary patients must agree to terms with the therapist before therapy can proceed.

Therapy, especially in institutional contexts, proceeds in stages (Korn and McCorkle 1959). In the first stage, there is a struggle for control, often passive and covert. The therapist is often tempted to become either autocratic or permissive. Neither approach is effective. It is important to establish boundaries and expectations without becoming punitive toward the client.

In the next stage of therapy, the client may express overt rebellion by refusing to come to sessions or participate in them. When this occurs, the counselor is advised to let the natural consequences of nonparticipation take their course rather than becoming too personally invested in getting the client to become involved. For example, when a probationer doesn't come to therapy, the counselor can advise the probation officer, then let whatever happens happen. If the benefits of counseling have been explained, then clients can deal with their decisions without exhortations from therapists.

Often clients must get sick and tired of being sick and tired before they agree to treatment. Alcoholism counselors refer to this as hitting the bottom or gutter. It is often hard to watch clients doing avoidable damage to themselves, but rescuing clients who don't want help is a form of co-dependency. Therapist, heal thyself.

After clients have run into the wall enough times, they may finally return to the therapist and ask for help. A sincere request for help makes it much easier to establish goals for treatment that both counselor and client can agree upon.

Points to Consider Regarding Treatment

Harris and Watkins (1987) describe the following helpful points for guiding the counseling process:

1. Counselors have to establish an environment in which communication can occur by looking at factors that facilitate and inhibit communication. Clients will not talk if they feel threatened, and most are more likely to talk if they sense the counselor's understanding.
2. The client's problem must be identified. What needs changing? What does the client think needs changing, if anything? What is blocking the change? Are there reasons why adapting would not be in the client's interest? Do the client's underlying character and values block normal relationships, or is the person capable of being influenced by feedback about the effect of his or her behavior on others?
3. Particularly with involuntary clients, counselors must understand and respond to impediments to change that arise as a result of the client's involuntary entrance into the counseling process. Does the client trust the counselor, or does he or she feel uncertain about disclosing information? Does the client doubt the value of counseling? Is the client angry at the

counselor because the counseling mandate was involuntary?
4. The counselor must select a counseling approach appealing to the style of the particular client. How does the client learn? Through action-oriented techniques? Through insight? Through talk about feelings? By seeing someone else perform the new behavior?
5. Counselors must understand the points at which their clients may be receptive to new understanding. What stage of treatment has the client reached? When should clients be confronted and when should they be allowed to "stew in their own juices?"
6. Counselors must develop an awareness of self and of organizational dynamics that hamper treatment. How can the counselor avoid inappropriate alliances with clients against other staff members? How can the counselor detect manipulation and respond therapeutically? Is the counselor responding appropriately to the client's transference, and is the counselor fully aware of his or her own counter-transference reaction?
7. Counselors must have some method to understand clients' tactics of resistance. How do clients evade personal responsibility by attacking or confusing the therapist? What is the best approach the counselor can use to respond effectively to these tactics from a particular client?

Counseling with difficult clients can be challenging and gratifying as well as draining and frustrating. Counselors need to evaluate whether their formal training is sufficient for understanding the problem of the help-rejecting client.

Fortunately, there is increasing attention in continuing education programs to therapeutic techniques for working with special populations, such as drug offenders, batterers, public offenders, socioeconomically deprived clients, and others.

Therapists have a professional obligation to continue beyond their academic training and think deeply about the practical problems that people face in our troubled world. Most therapists would have very few clients if they worked only with articulate and "motivated" clients. It is essential to develop skills to effectively counsel clients we call difficult.

References

Anderson, C., and S. Stewart. 1983. *Mastering resistance.* New York: Guilford Press.

Ansbacher, H. L. 1981. Prescott Lecky's concept of resistance and his personality. *Journal of Clinical Psychology* 37: 791-95.

Dowd, E., and C. Seibel. 1990. A cognitive theory of resistance and reactance: Implications for treatment. *Journal of Mental Health Counseling* 12(4):458-469.

Ellis, A. 1985. *Overcoming resistance.* New York: Springer.

Harris, G., and D. Watkins. 1987. *Counseling the involuntary and resistant client.* Laurel, Md.: American Correctional Association.

Korn, R., and L. McCorkle. 1959. *Criminology and penology.* New York: Rinehart and Winston.

Lyddon, W. 1990. First and second-order change: Implications for rationalist and constructivist cognitive therapies. *Journal of Counseling and Development* 69(2):122-127.

Meloy, R., A. Haroun, and E. Schiller. 1990. *Clinical guidelines for involuntary outpatient treatment.* Sarasota, Fla.: Professional Output Exchange.

Menninger, K. 1958. *Theory of psychoanalytic technique.* New York: Harper & Row.

Shertzer, B., and S. Stone. 1974. *Fundamentals of counseling.* Boston: Houghton Mifflin.

Weiss, J. 1990. Unconscious mental functioning. *Scientific American* (March):103-109.

Reproduced by permission. Copyright 1991, The Hatherleigh Co. Ltd., New York.

Some Practical Methods of Treating the Mandated Client

Jerry Larke

Pressure from an increasing number of societal concerns have resulted in the establishment of programs to identify and treat the sex offender, the child abuser, the alcohol and substance abuser, and others involved in the criminal justice system. These so-called resistant clients are seldom included in the typical mental health caseload. In fact, the absence of effective treatment methods and notoriously poor therapeutic outcomes are well documented (Goldstein 1973; Schofield 1964). Paradoxically, as more of these individuals are identified and mandated, or forced into accepting mental health treatment, there are extremely few mental health facilities or private practitioners available. The mental health practitioner has either little desire or feels inadequately trained to serve individuals with lifestyle problems. To compound the problem further, traditional mental health workers are taught that, for effective treatment to occur, clients must become involved of their own free will and "internally motivated to change" through their own efforts. This article presents some experience-based, practical methods of treating the compulsory client with an array of alternative methods targeted toward this population.

Despite the commonly held view that psychotherapy is primarily a middle- and upper-class activity, there exists ample evidence of attempts to modify treatment for the unmotivated client. In the area of family therapy, Salvadore Minuchin and his associates (1974) have focused on the therapy needs of inner-city minority clients. Goldstein (1973) developed structured learning therapy, a behavioral skill building approach, as psychotherapy for the poor. Anthony (1980) recommended teaching a repertoire of skills to enable the so-called rehabilitation or chronic client to cope more independently. Pepper (1982) recently reported on an innovative mental health program tailored to reach the young adult chronic client, a new group of "uninstitionalized" clients, who typically resist treatment until forced or coerced by legal authorities. Based on his experience, Pepper prefers that the young adult chronic client be on probation or referred as an alternative to jail, so more social controls and expectations can be placed on clients. A recent addition to the mental healthcare delivery system, the case manager, functions as informal therapist and often uses this relationship to entice resistant or noncompliant clients into appropriate treatment (Lamb 1979). Nontraditional clinics, such as walk-in centers, have also been used to attract the reluctant client into continuing drug maintenance (Anthony 1980). Van Putten (1982) suggested the direct teaching of the importance of compliance in chemotherapy with psychiatric clients.

However, the majority of literature citations deal with the obvious dilemmas of involuntary inpatient hospitalization (Dunham 1971; Liss and Allen 1975) and forced treatment of aggressive clients (Madden 1977). Except for case-specific psychoanalytic treatment (e.g., Bell and Hall 1971), minimal literature exists on outpatient treatment of sex offenders.

The bulk of studies involving compulsory treatment are found in the alcohol and substance abuse literature. The predominant finding seems to be that there exists little or no difference between mandated or voluntary clients vis-a-vis success at modifying alcohol use (Laundergan et al. 1979). In fact, some have found recidivism rates to be lower with the mandated population (Ward and Allivane 1979). These studies expose the "motivational myth" that voluntary clients appear at the outset to be desirous of treatment but tend to drop out when symptoms are reduced (marriage stability, regaining temper control, etc.). In contrast, the mandated client is forced to persist and may ultimately learn to be less fearful and resistant to treatment. Holser (1980) reported that, in the case of alcoholic clients, while in the process of getting their driver's license returned, a significant number became highly motivated to remain in treatment. Likewise, Dunham and Mause (1982) reported that coercive referral rendered successful treatment outcome considerably more likely than did the voluntary self-referral.

There also is some evidence that court-referred clients without an adjudication date are more resistant, violent, and poorer candidates than those with a hearing date. As a result, Rinella (1976) and Garrett (1981) recommended that only serious alcohol problems be mandated to intensive treatment, while less serious abusers be enrolled in educational programs. McGuire (1981) has studied the effectiveness of several drinking-driver programs and concluded that intensive and possibly long-term treatment be given the heavy abuser and less expensive countermeasures be developed for the light drinker. Recent ten-year follow-up studies of compulsory treatment after driving while intoxicated (DWI) convictions in California by Reis (1980, 1981) revealed that length of time in treatment was predictive of lowered recidivism rates; that is, treatment of at least one year or more was associated with permanent change.

In Western Europe there appears to be a greater tendency than in the United States to force criminal justice offenders, alcoholics, and sex offenders into treatment. Several authors contend successful outcome for such policies (Beltran-Ballester 1979; Milosovavic 1975). On the other hand, Norway seems to be decreasing in its reliance on mandated treatment while that country's suicide rate for the drug and alcohol abuser has risen. Nyhus (1979) draws a direct relationship between these two events. Armor et al. (1976) and Polick et al. (1980) in a review of alcohol treatment outcome studies concluded: (1) a majority of clients improved in life functioning as a result of treatment; (2) different types of treatment (individual, group, etc.) had no differential effects; but (3) treatment amount is the only variable having a significant effect outcome.

Assumptions about Treatment

The following are some useful assumptions that can assist the therapist in treating the compulsory client.

1. *Focused motivation.* Motivation for treatment does exist in the compulsory client although sometimes vague, compartmentalized, or unavailable. It is multifaceted and differentially reinforced. Motivation for what? is the relevant question. The client may well be motivated to work on return of his or her driver's license, completion of probation, or a positive report to family court. In short, identify the referent and motivation may be possible.
2. *Application of the borderline/narcissistic personality-disorder material.* The contribution of Kohut (1971, 1977) and Masterson (1982) seem especially useful with this population. (For an excellent review see Campbell, 1982.) Many mandated clients are fixated at a primitive level much like the borderline and typically use the seven primitive defenses of (1) avoidance, (2) acting-out, (3) denial, (4) clinging, (5) splitting, (6) projective identification, and (7) projection. Also one

or more of the four ego effects may exist: (1) low frustration tolerance, (2) poor impulse control, (3) poor ego functioning, and (4) diffuse ego boundaries.
3. *Awareness of fragile self-image.* Underlying a tough external shell exists a fragile self-image amenable to validation and acceptance by the therapist which enables the client to experience the self apart from the parent, spouse, or bottle. The result is the experiencing of the evolving self in a more independent, capable, and self-sufficient manner.
4. *Value of therapy.* In the context of compulsory treatment, psychotherapy is viewed as a seduction process with the goal being long-term treatment and follow-up care. The general strategy involves confronting the primitive defenses, validating the experience of the person, and focusing on separation/individuation issues. Equally important is the acquisition of concrete observable skills and the modeling of a quality relationship which may enable the client to overcome his or her fears of intimacy and closeness in an interpersonal relationship.
5. *Use of adjuncts.* The positive impact of traditional office therapy can be enhanced by the use of adjuncts to treatment (e.g., self-help groups such as Alcoholics Anonymous, Parents Anonymous, Recover, Inc., church, and other informal social support systems).
6. *Use of multimodel approach.* The use of a multimodel approach using behavioral contracting, the teaching of practical skills, and using homework seems most appropriate (Cautella 1980; Sheldon and Ackerman 1976). The focus of treatment should be on increasing competency and self-esteem, not verbally induced insight. An experiential knowledge of the culture of jails, prisons, and other institutions would also be helpful to the therapist. An open and frank review of the therapist's relevant work history can enhance competence with the skeptical client.

Alternative Treatment Methods

Pretreatment Structuring

Especially important to successful treatment of the mandated client is the establishment of clear, simple referral procedures. When the mental health worker decides to accept the mandated client for treatment, several critical, ethical issues must be clarified. As Chafetz (1965) said, if we are to protect the rights of the individual, compulsory treatment ought to be just one more technique in the caretaker's list of tools for enhancing motivation and needs we assume to exist in these clients. Fagan and Fagan (1982) speak of differentiating between a court referral and the legal coercion to keep the client in treatment. The task of the therapist is to maximize the quality of the referral by educating the referral source (the probation officer, lawyer, child-abuse worker, etc.) in the importance of administering treatment at a time when a person seems remorseful, depressed, or is verbalizing a desire to understand something about himself or herself. Within the legal system myths about mental health treatment are usually present. The therapist must help the referring agent have realistic expectations of treatment. It is important to explain that treatment is not punishment, nor should referrals be made in frustration or as a desperate maneuver.

Of course, frequency and duration of treatment, the estimated cost and how it is to be paid, common procedures used, and typical interim goals must be reviewed. The referral source needs to understand and support the concept that long-term treatment represents a viable alternative to deterrence methods and recidivism.

Behavioral Contracting and Time-limited Therapy

Of course the benefits of behavioral contracting with the psychotherapy client are well known. However, to the mandated client, behavioral contracting forms the essential cornerstone of treatment. At the first meeting, there is an attempt made to set the atmosphere of subsequent meetings of modeling honesty, openness, directness, and respect. The client is told that the medical record has not been read in advance so as to avoid prejudice and preconceived opinions. The following items of confidentiality are stressed:

1. All contacts from others must have prior approval of the client at each contact. This would include employer, family member, judge, and lawyer, and whether a release was signed or not. Explain that only a court of record can legally request the medical record. Clients get copies of all reports to courts, lawyers, judges, etc.
2. At each session, all contacts of the previous week are discussed.

3. Offer to review the medical record and case notes with the client to establish trust.
4. Finally, stress the importance of independence and distance from the referral source and the role of therapist as a helper to individuals and as a person who can help them to avoid or prevent future problems.

Next, treatment goals are formulated to establish the purpose for meeting. Mandated clients often establish such goals as regaining custody of their children, successful completion of parole, or securing a positive recommendation for return of a driver's license. As a potent incentive, positive reports are sent to the legal authorities documenting client consistency (i.e., keeping appointments, completing homework assignments, attending AA, PA meetings). The majority of behavioral interventions used are from Cautella (1980), Sheldon and Ackerman (1976), and Wallace (1978). Treatment plans are then signed by both client and therapist, and reviewed at regular intervals.

At session one, client and therapist expectations are set establishing the appointment time. In order to model consistency and reliability, the therapist should establish an inflexible, scheduled appointment time. This is especially important in establishing a relationship with clients whose parental figures were unreliable. The process of cancellation and the consequences of missed meetings are reviewed. Usually after the first missed meeting, the client is confronted via telephone. If the second meeting is missed, the client is forced to wait and resume treatment after others on the waiting list have begun. The referral source is informed after the second delinquency. Frequency and duration of treatment are established, usually weekly in the beginning and for nine months to one year in duration. Review of cost and method of payment is done at this time.

The gathering of an in-depth social history allows the client to begin verbal ventilation of past unpleasant events, and the therapist encourages ventilation about the frustrations of coping with the pressures of life. Some special issues to explore are the failure of past treatment attempts, relationship failures, the client's view of the arrest record, work history and training, and the relationship of drug and/or alcohol abuse to antisocial behavior.

Time-limited therapy offers many advantages to the mandated client. After a thorough discussion of the benefits and liabilities of long-term treatment, the client will often settle down and accept, even if in a passive compliant manner, the course of treatment. Since many display impaired ego functioning (low frustration tolerance and poor impulse control particularly), the setting of a termination date can help them learn patience and tolerance. Another hidden benefit of long-term time-limited therapy is the trying out of a new role, much in the spirit of Kelly's (1955) fixed-role therapy. Due to the length of time in the new role, the client may learn to feel some ownership and identity with this new set of behaviors. An example would be the problem drinker abstaining from alcohol, or the child abuser enrolling in a developmental psychology course and writing weekly reports on experiences. This "artificial" transformation may provide sufficient dissonance for the client to begin working through the resistance to trying out a new identity.

Application of Kohut's Self-psychology and Masterson's Borderline Conditions Approaches

Overlooking the theoretical inconsistencies and disagreements within the borderline conditions literature, one can readily adapt many of these methods to treatment of the mandated client. Psychodynamically, many persons who comprise the mandated client category are viewed as being primitively fixated in the separation/individuation phase of development (Masterson 1982). As a result, the primitive defenses of denial, acting-out, avoidance, clinging, projection, projective identification, and splitting are in constant operation defending the fragile, frightened self. Masterson also assumes that the four ego defects (low frustration tolerance, poor ego functioning, diffuse ego boundaries, and poor impulse control) may also exist. Both Kohut and Masterson believe the establishment of a trusting relationship is the key to facilitating change. Masterson believes the borderline triad of separation/individuation failure produces an abandonment depression which is primitively defended. The therapeutic task is to confront the primitive defenses when they occur causing the person to experience this abandonment depression and begin the working-through process of understanding his or her failure at individuating. Masterson has recently revised his work to recommend two types of treatment—confrontive/supportive and reconstructive. Confrontive/supportive therapy is the treatment of choice for people who are unable, or are in too much pain, to work through their fixations and must adapt to society and function realistically.

Kohut (1971, 1977), on the other hand, recommends that the therapist validate the individual's dilemmas or frustrations with life, thereby regulating the client's self-esteem. The therapist is to show great empathy for the plight of the person. This narcissistic entitlement provides a positive atmosphere for the person to explore the hurt and anger of often being downtrodden by society—family, friends, fellow workers, and social agencies. The quest here is to mutually search and discover the positive or good self and help the person internalize this image along with the negative self which forms an integrated whole. The therapist can encourage the ventilation of negative feelings and help the client release anger and rage. This basic orientation works well with mandated clients since in their environment few people are often sympathetic or understanding. The therapist is a contrast to the more punitively-oriented legal authorities and can encourage the client's rejection of the social stigma associated with the act or crime. From experience one can assume that no one cherishes the stigma of society's outcasts—sex offenders, criminals, substance abusers. It can also be assumed that the client desires to shed this negative self-image if only he or she know how. An open discussion of the point usually is productive. Therapy sessions can function to successfully regulate the client's self-esteem around this important issue.

Family Therapy with One Person

Another practical method that can favorably affect mandated clients is the use of family therapy with the identified client (Bowen 1978). Often the resistant client will not bring the spouse/girl/boy/friend into treatment even though it was agreed upon at the outset. A common angry attitude expressed is, "It's my problem, so I'll pay for it." "It doesn't involve her." Rather than engage in a power struggle, the therapist may choose to teach the client to relate better with the spouse or other family members by assigning relationship tasks to be completed by the client between sessions. A client might, for example, decide to talk to his or her parents about their marriage.

Then client and therapist are free to explore such questions as: What is the attitude of the mate toward the offense or toward the client? Has there been an increase in family tension? In spite of the generally accepted family therapy tenet of the importance of involving the mate in treatment, the therapist may find it more productive to work with each mate separately and avoid a mutually denying or resisting couple.

Use of Peer Support Groups

The potency of peer support or self-help groups is well known (Reisman and Gardiner 1977). However, the historical problems between professional mental health workers and self-help groups such as Alcoholics Anonymous and Recovery, Inc., are also documented (Zimberg et al. 1978). Katz and Ralde (1981) studied "treatment packages" where traditional psychotherapy and alternative self-help groups were employed simultaneously, sequentially, or in alternation. Some clients transformed the apparent conflict into complementary and mutually enhancing help from different non-overlapping sources. In the experience of the author, it is possible to work out positive and independent areas of clinical responsibility. For example, attendance at AA would assist the client with his or her drinking problem, freeing up the therapist to focus attention on separation/individuation issues and life-functioning concerns. Since many of these individuals are socially isolated, they receive little opportunity for companionship—or "twinship" in Kohut's terminology—and the discovery that they are not alone in this plight. The client also has the opportunity to observe positive social models similar to himself or herself who have been successful in changing targeted behaviors, made progress in their legal difficulties, and acquired more positive attitudes toward their lives. Of course, the therapist has the obligation to be very knowledgeable about the self-help groups that his or her clients have been asked to attend. Only through the therapy relationship can the therapist be assured that the client is learning and progressing, as formal referrals cannot be made to self-help groups.

In the last three months of treatment, meetings are usually held monthly and are referred to as "aftercare" sessions. The focus is on (1) a discussion of homework assignments (pleasant events forms, self-control monitoring sheets, etc.), (2) report of regular attendance at peer support groups, and (3) a review of personal and family gains (a vacation, a savings account, a remodeled room, better use of leisure time, social contacts, etc.). During these last meetings, the spouse/girl/boy/friend is asked to be involved to enhance learning transfer and reinforce persistence.

Special Treatment Issues

In order to successfully treat the mandated client, an array of therapist-specific issues must be considered. The therapist's role must be active and not passive. Mandated clients need a reality ego and real objects to guide them successfully through "new" social situations rather than resorting to old counterproductive, antisocial solutions. Also, the submissive therapist's failure to confront leads clients to feel that the therapist does not care. In fact, clients may feel that the therapist is dependent, needs approval, and fears the clients' tendency to act out. The denigration of the therapist's potency must be resisted at all costs, keeping in mind that the borderline and many mandated clients see the therapist as "enemy" and convenient scapegoat. [See Masterson (1982) for a comprehensive discussion of this point.] Another important contributor to the therapist's self-denigration is capitulating to the pressures of the client. Such an example would be to modify the treatment contract significantly by ending treatment early or the premature approval for a driver's license.

In order to work successfully with this population, the therapist must combat the tendency to consciously or unconsciously give up on the therapeutic relationship. The actual presentation of the client's personality—which is often hostile, angry, unappreciative, or manipulative—provides ample justification or unconscious motivation to discontinue treatment. However, the therapist needs to recall the probable primitive fixation of these clients and refocus his or her attention on positive, observable gains in order to save the relationship from self-destruction.

Finally, the therapist must devote ample time to planning the intervention strategy for each resistant client. Regular clinical case consultation or peer supervision is helpful because the loss of objectivity is especially predictable.

The therapist must be flexible in the treatment approach and be prepared to change direction if and when needed.

References

Anthony, W. A. 1980. *The principles of psychiatric rehabilitation*. Baltimore: University Park Press.

Arbor, D. J., J. M. Polick, and H. B. Stanbul. 1976. *Alcohol and treatment*. Santa Monica, Calif.: Rand Corporation.

Bell, A.P., and C. S. Hobb. 1971. *The personality of a child molester*. Chicago: Aldine.

Beltran-Ballester, E. 1979. Drugs and the penal law. *Drogalcohol* 4:169-183.

Bowen, M. 1978. *Family therapy in clinical practice*. New York: Jason Aronson.

Campbell, K. 1982. The psychotherapy relationship with

borderline personality disorders. *Psychotherapy: Theory, Research and Practice* 19(2):166-193.

Cautella, J. R. 1980. *Behavioral analysis: Forms for clinical intervention, Vol. I.* Champaign, Ill.: Research Press.

Chafetz, M. E. 1965. Is compulsory treatment of the alcoholic effective? *Northwest Medicine* 64:932-937.

Dunham, H. W. 1971. Legalized compulsory treatment for psychiatric illness. *American Journal of Public Health* 61(6):1076-1079.

Dunham, R. G., and A. L. Mauss. 1982. Reluctant referrals: The effectiveness of legal coercion in outpatient treatment for public drinkers. *Journal of Drug Issues* 12(1):5-20.

Fagan, R. W., and N. M. Fagan. 1982. Impact of legal coercion on the treatment of alcoholism. *Journal of Drug Issues* 12(1):103-117.

Garrett, J. A. 1981. Adjustment demand: Resistance to alcoholism treatment with DWI population. In L. Goldberg (ed.), *Drugs and Traffic Safety, Vol. III*, pp. 1429-1445.

Goldstein, A. P. 1973. *Structured learning therapy: Towards psychotherapy for the poor.* New York: Academic.

Holser, M. A. 1980. *Motivational myths, the mandated client and the volunteer: A comparison of alcohol programs for mandated clients and volunteer clients—an opinion survey.* Lane County Council of Alcoholism, Eugene, Oregon (whole).

Katz, R., and E. Ralde. 1981. Community alternatives to psychotherapy. *Psychotherapy: Theory, Research and Practice* 18(3):365-374.

Kelly, G. 1955. *The psychology of personal constructs.* New York: W. W. Norton.

Kohut, H. 1971. *The analysis of the self.* New York: International Universities Press.

Kohut, H. 1977. *The restoration of the self.* New York: International Universities Press.

Lamb, H. R. 1980. Therapist—case managers: More than brokers of service. *Hospital and Community Psychiatry* 31:762-764.

Laundegan, J. C., J. W. Spicer, and N. L. Krammerer. 1979. *Are court referrals effective?* Center City, Minn.: Hazledon Foundation.

Liss, R., and F. A. Allen. 1975. Court mandated treatment: Dilemmas for hospital psychiatry. *American Journal of Psychiatry* 132(9):924-927.

Madden, D. J. 1977. Voluntary and involuntary treatment of aggressive patients. *American Journal of Psychiatry* 124(5):553-555.

Masterson, J. F. 1982. *The narcissistic and borderline disorders*. New York: Brunner/Mazel.

McGuire, F. L. 1981. Social action and the current state of knowledge in treating drinking drivers. *Abstracts and Reviews in Alcohol and Driving* 2(1):11-13.

Milosavcevic, V. 1975. Compulsory treatment of alcoholism. *Alkoholizam Beograd* 15(1-2):112-115.

Minuchin, S. 1974. *Families and family therapy*. Cambridge, Mass.: Harvard University Press.

Nyhus, P. 1979. Right to compulsory treatment—a possibility of misuse. *Tidsski Edrusporsm* 31(1):3-16.

Pepper, B. 1982. The impact of uninstitutionalization on a CMHC: A systems perspective. Paper presented at the annual meeting of National Community Mental Health Centers, New York, March 11.

Polick, M. J., P. J. Armor, and H. B. Braiker. 1980. *The course of alcoholism: Four years after treatment*. Santa Monica, Calif.: Rand Corporation.

Reisman, F., and A. Gartner. 1977. *Self help in the human services*. San Francisco: Jossey-Bass.

Reis, R. E., and L. A. Lewis. 1980. First interim analysis of multiple offender treatment effectiveness. County of Sacramento Health Department, Office of Alcoholism, California.

Reis, R. E. 1981. Effectiveness of education and treatment programs for drinking drivers: A decade of evaluation. In L. Goldberg (ed.), *Alcohol, Drugs and Traffic Safety, Vol. III*, pp. 1298-1328.

Rinella, V. J. 1976. Rehabilitation or bust: The impact of criminal justice system referrals on the treatment of drug addicts and alcoholics in a therapeutic community. *American Journal of Drug and Alcohol Abuse* 3(1):53-58.

Schofield, W. 1964. *Psychotherapy: The purchase of friendship*. Englewood Cliffs, N. J.: Prentice-Hall.

Sheldon, J. L., and J. M. Ackerman. 1976. *Homework in counseling and psychotherapy*. Springfield, Ill.: Charles C Thomas.

Van Putten, J. 1982. Dealing with noncompliance in the schizophrenic outpatient. *Schizophrenic Outpatient* 1(2):1-5.

Wallace, J. 1978. Behavioral modification methods as adjuncts to psychotherapy. In S. Zimberg, J. Wallace, and S.

Blume (eds.), *Practical approaches to alcoholism psychotherapy.* New York: Plenum, pp. 99-116.

Ward, D. A., and K. J. Allivane. 1979. Effects of legal coercion on the treatment of alcohol related criminal offenders. *Justice System Journal* 5(1):107-11.

Zimberg, S., J. Wallace, and S. B. Blum. (eds.) 1978. *Practical approaches to alcoholism psychotherapy.* New York: Plenum.

Reprinted from Psychotherapy 22(2):262-268. *Used by permission.*

Identifying and Confronting Resistance in Lifestyle Criminal Offenders

Glenn D. Walters

Offender populations are resistant and involuntary almost by definition. Whether we encounter the criminal in a correctional facility or community setting, it is rare to find more than a handful of such individuals in search of genuine behavioral change. Most arrive at the psychologist's or counselor's office with designs of obtaining special consideration, which might include requests for single cell placement or a favorable parole recommendation in an institutional setting or demands for a positive bill of mental health to satisfy a spouse, employer, or judge in a community setting. Regardless of the motivation, the offender's presence in the counselor's office is the first step in the intervention process, a step that can be capitalized on if the therapist knows how to effectively deal with the offender's resistance to long-term behavioral change.

A primary cause of an offender's resistance to change can be found in the fact that crime is often a highly reinforcing behavior capable of providing near-immediate payoffs. Instead of waiting six months to accrue funds sufficient to purchase an automobile, some offenders will conveniently rob a bank or store, pay for the car in cash, and bypass the necessity (and hassle) of securing a loan or making monthly payments. Rather than trying to work out a disagreement, there are offenders who will belittle, verbally assault, or—in extreme cases—do physical harm to persons with whom they do not get along. In order to combat the immediate gratification of criminal activity, counselors and therapists must endeavor to point out the long-term destructiveness of criminal conduct and work to expose the erroneous roots of this behavior (i.e., criminal thinking).

It is important to understand that, like trees, there are many different varieties of criminal. The class of criminal offender to which this paper is directed is a group that approaches crime as a lifestyle rather than as a series of isolated or nonintegrated behaviors. Research suggests that while such individuals comprise only a small percentage of the total criminal population, they account for a majority of the serious crimes committed each year (Chaiken and Chaiken 1982; Figgie Corporation 1988; Hamparian et al. 1978; Shannon 1982; Wolfgang, Sellin, and Figlio 1972). This should not be taken to mean that non-lifestyle patterns of lawbreaking behavior are completely unrelated to habitual patterns of criminal conduct, just that the emphasis here will be on the lifestyle pattern. For whether we are talking about trees or criminals, the many varieties have certain properties and characteristics in common.

Defining the Criminal Lifestyle

The lifestyle criminal is one who has developed a lifestyle characterized by four principle behaviors: irresponsibility, self-indulgence, interpersonal intrusiveness, and social rule breaking (Walters 1990). The irresponsibility demonstrated by the average lifestyle criminal is habitual and characterologic rather than isolated and circumscribed. The lifestyle criminal's self-indulgence is testimony to the fact that he or she lacks self-restraint and is willing to sacrifice long-term success in exchange for immediate gratification.

Substance abuse, sexual promiscuity, and gambling are several of the more common manifestations of self-indulgence as observed in the typical lifestyle offender. Interpersonal intrusiveness, on the other hand, is expressed in violations of others' rights, freedoms, or personal space and is reflected in crimes like murder, rape, and robbery, although certain categories of property crime (e.g., burglary, breaking and entering) also display features of an interpersonally intrusive nature. Finally, the prototypic lifestyle criminal has spent a great deal of time circumventing the rules of his or her parents, the norms of the community, and the laws of society—a pattern that normally begins in early adolescence. Whether this entails stealing money from a mother's purse, getting suspended from school for skipping detention, or being picked up by the police for shoplifting, the social rule breaking activities of the lifestyle criminal continually bring him or her into conflict with the norms of the wider society.

Subdividing the correlates of criminality into conditions, choice, and cognition can be a useful way to understand the development of lifestyle patterns of criminal conduct. The conditions of one's life can be either internal (genetics, intelligence, temperament) or external (physical environment, family atmosphere, peer relationships) and serve to increase or decrease one's future risk for criminal involvement. There is abundant research to suggest that certain factors, among them heredity (Walters and White 1989a), a difficult temperament (Kellam et al. 1982), and drug abuse (Ball, Shaffer, and Nurco 1983), may increase one's chances of becoming involved in serious criminality. Other conditions, including above average intelligence (Kandel et al. 1988), a positive relationship with one or more parent (Werner and Smith 1977), and positive social association with peers (Osborn and West 1980), may tend to insulate otherwise vulnerable youth from involving themselves in a life of crime. Though conditions do not cause crime directly, they do appear to enhance or diminish one's chances of developing along criminal lines.

If conditions do not determine criminality, what does? Once we develop the ability to think and reason, even at a rudimentary level, choice is what determines behavior, criminal or otherwise. Except in the case of extreme mental or emotional disability, most people have attained the capacity to choose, although this ability develops with both age and experience. Under most circumstances, then, we would not hold a five-year-old child legally responsible for killing a playmate, though we nearly always hold twenty-five-year-olds culpable of such an act. This is because an adult is more capable of comprehending the nature of murder as a function of both neurocognitive development and increased exposure to a wider sphere of experience. Unlike the typical five-year-old, who is largely dependent on his or her immediate environment (nuclear family) for information about the world, adults have had greater contact with extra-familial sources of information through contacts in school and in the neighborhood as well as through exposure to media. Consequently, adults typically have more options available to them than most children.

When conditions restrict our options, choice determines which options we use. Ultimately, the selection process itself is influenced by factors external to the individual. However, it is a fundamental tenet of the lifestyle theory of criminal involvement that the human decision makers always have the option of avoiding old reinforcement patterns and responding to new ones. If this were not true, behavioral continuity would be nearly absolute and change would be all but impossible.

To support his or her life choices, the individual constructs a cognitive system capable of justifying, rationalizing, and perpetuating the lifestyle upon which these choices are predicated. Developmental and experiential factors are of prime importance in understanding this thinking style. Lifestyle criminals' development differs from that of their noncriminal peers in the sense that they actively avoid maturity, responsibility, and other early precursors of adult development. Experientially, lifestyle criminals are reinforced for criminal behavior because they see that it leads to immediate gratification, although as a result of immaturity they fail to take into account the negative long-term consequences of their behavior and the thinking on which this behavior is based. The thinking of lifestyle criminals can be defined by eight patterns of irrational thought. (See Table 1.)

Resistance and the Lifestyle Criminal

Resistance is commonly defined as opposing, contesting, or withstanding the ideas, actions, or wishes of another. The lifestyle criminal has spent a lifetime opposing the ideas, actions, and wishes of others, although he or she resists change most of all. Changing thoughts and behaviors that have become the sustenance of one's lifestyle can be both frightening and difficult.

Over the course of violating the laws of society and the personal rights of others, the lifestyle criminal has formed a protective shield of justifications, rationalizations, and excuses. Nullifying this resistance will require a maximum degree of patience and commitment on the part of the therapist or counselor. This will involve dealing with resistance at the following three levels:

- resistance based on the conditions of one's life
- resistance based on the choices one has made and continues to make relative to these conditions
- resistance based on the thinking style that has evolved in support of the choices one has made relative to the criminal lifestyle

Condition-based Resistance

Conditions are factors that we must learn to either accept, circumvent, or in a few cases change (e.g., drug usage). Many lifestyle criminals sabotage their treatment by focusing their attention on life conditions and complaining that they never had a chance to make something of themselves. The therapist must be careful to avoid reinforcing this thinking, for there is too little to be gained from taking a precursory approach to criminal development. The prison or jail environment also lends itself to certain counter-therapeutic influences in the sense that the offender is surrounded by other criminals, many of whom encourage conflict with society and preservation of old criminal thinking patterns. Walters and White (1988) discuss several ways in which the correctional environment might be made more effective for the purposes of teaching attributes and skills the lifestyle criminal lacks (e.g., responsibility, self-restraint, interpersonal problem solving ability). However, we must avoid protracted discussions of such issues in our clinical work with offenders since it can easily divert attention from the task at hand, which in this instance is helping offenders to change their behavior by changing their thinking.

To limit condition-based resistance, the therapist should listen attentively, be straightforward, and make it clear to the lifestyle offender that change is possible. What sets the lifestyle approach to intervention with high-rate offenders apart from the more traditional forms of psychotherapy is that it places a premium on the direct application of cognitive and behavioral principles, is largely didactic in nature, and sees the value of confrontation as a means of promoting behavioral change. The emphasis of this system of intervention is on the here and now rather than on the past, and the therapist using such an approach is encouraged to challenge sundry aspects of criminal thought without being overly critical or judgmental. Hence, where an offender might claim that he or she was a victim of nefarious personal and social conditions, the therapist or counselor will want to point out that this statement is founded on assumptions the individual may want to examine more closely.

Choice-based Resistance

A major impediment to change in lifestyle criminals is the belief that they had no choice but to engage in the criminal act that led to their current charges or confinement. The culprit might be poverty, peers, drugs, or an unfortunate home environment, but rarely do offenders blame themselves for what they have done. Some criminals will pay lip service to the idea that they were responsible for their actions, although a careful review of their statements will typically reveal rationalizations and excuses interspliced with assertions that they are responsible for their criminality. This is because lifestyle criminals must deceive themselves before they can deceive others. They have invested large amounts of time and energy in constructing a system of justification that does not simply disappear once they are arrested or incarcerated.

In confronting choice-based resistance it is essential that the major choices the offender has made in life be reviewed and that the individual be made to realize that events do not occur haphazardly. Therefore, while conditions most certainly influence behavior, they do not determine it. To understand how behavior is determined, we need to consider choice and decision making. Monahan (1973) cites research that demonstrates that people who view themselves as responsible for their actions are among the more successful and contributing members of the community. Showing offenders where their lives have gone awry because of criminal thinking and poor decision making, much in the manner described by Samenow (1984), is critical in tackling choice-based resistance. If properly conducted, such a technique can become a vital link in the offender's search for future behavioral change since it is difficult, even for the most hardened criminals, to ignore the fact that they have little to show for their years of fast living.

The initial stages of intervention with choice-based resistance are probably best handled in individual sessions with a trained counselor or therapist. However, once initial resistance has been eclipsed, the more subtle and entrenched features of choice-based resistance can probably best be managed with group therapy. Such groups provide the offender with a great wealth of new information gleaned from interactions with other individuals who also have a personal understanding of the criminal lifestyle. It also provides for the formation of an external challenging mechanism (offenders challenging each other) with the prospect of internalization somewhere down the line. In fact, implementation of an internalized challenging mechanism is the primary goal of the lifestyle approach to intervention.

Cognition-based Resistance

Since resistance is largely a cognitive phenomenon, it should come as no surprise that it can probably be most effectively managed at the cognitive or self-talk level. The resistance observed at this level is rooted in the irrationality of the criminal lifestyle as represented by the eight thinking patterns listed and briefly described in Table 1. This cognitive system arises as a means of buttressing the lifestyle offender's criminal decisions, thereby allowing the individual to resist more rational thoughts that, if realized, would threaten the survival of his or her lifestyle. Techniques and procedures designed to confront the irrationality of cognition-based resistance are manifold and will be examined individually for each of the eight patterns. Where possible, specific examples of cognition-based resistance, along with suggestions on how one might intervene with the lifestyle criminal, will be provided.

Mollification

The excuses and justifications that subserve mollification are a prime target for early interventions with the lifestyle criminal. Offenders will often direct their resistance to concerns about unfairness or societal injustice, or they may express their mollification by blaming the victim or minimizing the seriousness of their past criminal acts. No matter what form it assumes, mollification must be challenged; as long as it is allowed to continue, the offender will spend his or her time projecting blame onto the external environment rather than accepting responsibility for his or her actions and taking an honest look at him or herself. What follows are a few examples of cognition-based resistance expressed through mollification.

MOL-1: "What happened to me was not fair!"

Comment: Unfairness is in the eye of the beholder. What is unfair to one person may be more than fair to another. Moreover, inequity is something that has always existed and, unfortunately, probably always will. Consequently, demanding that life be fair is not only arrogant, but also unrealistic. This does not mean we must simply accept situations we believe to be unjust, though we also needn't spend endless amounts of time ruminating about things over which we have no control.

MOL-2: "The police (FBI, DEA) did not play by their own rules in arresting me!"

Comment: Simply stated, two wrongs don't make a right. This awareness does little to deter lifestyle criminals, however. They may spend hours struggling to justify their wrongful behavior by pointing out that some of those charged with the responsibility of upholding the laws of society are either breaking these laws or engaging in unethical conduct. What lifestyle criminals need to realize is that what other people do has nothing to do with them and that they cannot use others' misconduct, perceived or real, to excuse their own violations of the law.

MOL-3: "Everyone does it; I just happened to get caught."

Comment: Chances are everyone else is not doing it. This simply speaks to lifestyle criminals' tendency to think in extremes and highlights their limited experience with the world in that they believe everyone else thinks and acts as they do. If, by chance, others were to engage in illegal activities with the voracity and dedication of the lifestyle criminal, chances are they too would find themselves spending inordinate amounts of time in jail and prison.

MOL-4: "The victim deserved what he (she) got!"

Comment: Rarely does a victim ask for what the lifestyle criminal dishes out. Although some victims may not have been as vigilant as they might have been guarding against the possibility of becoming a victim of crime, this in no way excuses, mitigates, or abates the severity of the high rate offender's predatory behavior. Such a statement is nothing more than a smokescreen lifestyle criminals use to cloud the vision of both themselves and others.

Cutoff

Confronting the cutoff involves challenging the impulsiveness that characterizes the criminal lifestyle. As such, self-restraint and frustration tolerance are both antithetical to the cutoff. Lifestyle offenders will apply the cutoff in order to avoid the responsibilities associated with future emotional development. Consequently, they never learn to deal with situations in a mature manner—they just "blow their top," and others characteristically give in to their demands. While this approach may be effective in the short run, it creates problems for habitual lawbreakers in the long run. This may include prison, divorce, or retaliation, but it is certain to be negative. Illustrating the long-term negative consequences of cutoff-mediated resistance is crucial to the success of any future interventions with lifestyle criminals.

In discussing the cutoff, it is important to distinguish between the internal cutoff and external cutoff. An internal cutoff is a word, phrase, image, or musical theme that is employed by the lifestyle offender to eliminate common deterrents to criminal action. In confronting the internal cutoff it is vital that the therapist teach offenders to challenge their thinking by asking themselves:

1. Is the cutoff based on a rational understanding of the current situation?
2. Will the action that ensues from the cutoff result in the achievement of both short- and long-range goals?

External cutoffs are exterior objects introduced by the criminal to deflate or eliminate deterrents to crime. Drugs and alcohol are by far the most common form of external cutoff. External cutoffs are best challenged by avoiding situations and objects (e.g., drugs, pornography) that have been known to fuel cutoff thoughts and feelings in that particular offender.

Entitlement

Lifestyle offenders tell themselves that they are entitled to take things that don't belong to them, violate the laws of society, and intrude on the personal lives of others. They accomplish this by extending personal ownership to others' property, convincing themselves of their own uniqueness, and misidentifying wants as needs. The following are several examples of entitlement-based resistance and how one might proceed with offenders who express such sentiments:

ENT-1: "But I'm different."

Comment: Many lifestyle criminals conclude relatively early in life that they are unique, special people for whom the laws of society do not apply. However, as they find themselves continually in trouble with the law—including regular trips to jail and prison—reality gradually begins to set in. Hence, it is not uncommon to see entitlement-based resistance, as manifest by protestations of one's uniqueness, decline with age. A principle goal of intervention is to bring this awareness to younger offenders who may have not come to this realization on their own.

ENT-2: "Society owes me!"

Comment: This sentiment is particularly strong after an offender is released from prison after serving a multiyear sentence. Such individuals act as if it were society's fault they have spent the last several years in prison. They conclude that society "owes" them and that if they can't get what they want legally, they will take it. While there is nothing wrong with pursuing legitimate opportunities in the community, in order to achieve lasting success habitual criminals must adopt the attitude that society owes them nothing. From this point, they can then begin building a new life for themselves.

ENT-3: "I need a new house (late-model car, expensive jewelry, drugs)."

Comment: Basic human needs include requirements for air, food, water, shelter, and, in some cases, clothing; everything else is viewed as a want or desire. However, the lifestyle criminal grants himself or herself permission to violate the laws of society and the personal dignity of others by elevating his or her wants for a variety of personal, material, and luxury items to the status of needs. This is a major component of cognition-based resistance in that as long as the offender believes he or she needs these material goods, he or she will continue to violate the law in order to obtain these goods. These material goods constitute wants, not needs, and the individual is not justified in pursuing them at any cost.

Power Orientation

Environmental control is a predominant theme in the behavioral armamentation of the average lifestyle criminal. When lifestyle offenders are not in control of their immediate environment, they characteristically experience what Yochelson and Samenow (1976) call a zero state. Criminals who find themselves in the depths of a zero state believe themselves to be helpless, hopeless, and impotent. In order to shake themselves free of zero state feelings, lifestyle offenders will engage in what Yochelson and Samenow refer to as a power thrust. The power thrust involves putting someone else down physically, emotionally, or mentally so that the offender feels more in control of the situation. What follows are several additional ways offenders use the power orientation to resist change and how an offender experiencing a zero state or engaging in a power thrust can be more effectively managed.

POW-1: "People are either weak or strong."

Comment: Lifestyle offenders hold to the oversimplified view of people as either weak or strong, and because of their preoccupation with external control they value physical muscle over mental virility. It is essential that the validity of this belief be vigorously challenged since it provides one more example of how lifestyle criminals use their thinking to avoid new information and resist the prospect of change.

POW-2: "I'm a zero."

Comment: Lifestyle criminals are no more zeros than they are all-powerful. However, they must separate themselves from this all-or-nothing thinking if they are to extricate themselves from the criminal lifestyle that now envelopes their behavior. To accomplish this goal, habitual offenders must abandon their exclusive reliance on an external interpretation of events, for only then will they truly be able to avoid zero state feelings and the impulse to power thrust in situations over which they have little external control.

POW-3: "I'm right and you're wrong!"

Comment: A power-oriented individual may resist change by throwing up an angry facade designed to keep the therapist or counselor at bay. The therapist might want to redirect the conversation to the issues at hand, asking the offender, "If it is true that you are so knowledgeable about this subject, why is it that you have spent so much of your adult life confined in various jails and prisons?" It is critical that we provide the lifestyle criminal engaged in power thrusting behavior the opportunity to reflect on him or herself and on the desire to be in control of his or her environment. Only then can the resistance posed by the drive to win at all costs be reduced to a level where the individual can benefit from treatment.

Sentimentality

The "good guy" image the lifestyle criminal has etched of himself or herself is one more factor that impedes future behavioral change. High-rate offenders reason that engaging in certain positive behaviors somehow exonerates them of their past criminality. As is the case with all forms of cognition-based resistance, if we do not directly confront the sentimentality, change cannot occur. This is because offenders reason that as long as they do good deeds, they are okay, their behavior is okay, and so there is no need for change. What follows are several examples of sentimentality-based resistance and possible ways of dealing with each.

SEN-1: "I've never hurt anyone."

Comment: The problem with this statement is that the lifestyle criminal is probably using a self-servingly narrow definition of harm. What the offender means is that he or she has never harmed anyone physically. However, psychological and emotional harm can be just as debilitating as physical harm. Entering a bank wielding weapons and shouting obscenities will probably create emotional turmoil for bank employees and patrons alike, causing nightmares, anxiety, and interpersonal difficulties that may last longer than the bank robber's prison sentence. In saying that he or she has never inflicted injury while committing a crime, the lifestyle criminal is discounting the psychological and emotional harm this behavior has caused friends, family, and himself or herself. The lifestyle criminal offender must become aware of the damage this antisocial behavior brings and then use this to stimulate future behavioral change.

SEN-2: "I'm a normal person with normal ideas, drives, and goals."

Comment: Psychologists have struggled for decades with the issue of defining normality. What they have discovered is that normality defies definition except within very wide parameters. Most lifestyle criminals are normal to the extent that they are free of serious emotional disorders. However, their behavior is far enough outside the bounds of conventionality that society has deemed it necessary to segregate them from the rest of the population. Unlike many of their victims, lifestyle criminals have a choice—they can live according to the rules of society and remain free in the community, or they can violate these rules and spend much of the rest of their lives in jail or prison.

SEN-3: "What's wrong with doing nice things for others?"

Comment: There is nothing wrong with doing nice things for others. There is, however, something very wrong with using one's record of "good deeds" to perpetuate a lifestyle that victimizes others for the sake of the offender's self-gratification.

Superoptimism

The resistance provided by superoptimism is reflected in the fact that lifestyle criminals never seriously contemplate change because they believe they will be able to avoid the long-term consequences of their criminal behavior. If because of irresponsibility and financial mismanagement lifestyle criminals find themselves short of funds, they may rob a store or burglarize a home, confident that the police will never apprehend them. If they do get caught, they resist change by convincing themselves that they will beat the case. If convicted they will likely deceive themselves further by superoptimistically banking on a sentence reduction or parole. What follows are two additional examples of how lifestyle criminals use superoptimism to resist behavioral change.

SUP-1: "No matter what, I'll get away."

Comment: Lifestyle criminals' superoptimistic attitude is based on past experience. Nearly all lifestyle criminals have gotten away with the majority of their crimes. This is because the American system of jurisprudence is more concerned that the innocent be protected than that the guilty be prosecuted. The problem with lifestyle criminals is that their criminal actions are so repetitive (sometimes to the point of victimizing the same person, house, or store) that they eventually get caught. Until high rate offenders realize the self-destructive nature of their superoptimism, they will continue to resist change because they are operating on the mistaken belief that they can get away with just about any crime.

SUP-2: In referring to jail or prison, the lifestyle criminal may retort, "This is nothing."

Comment: Like most reflections of superoptimism, this statement is partially true, although distorted. Most recidivistic lawbreakers first encounter jail at a relatively early age and commonly report that they were surprised to learn that jail was not as uncomfortable as they had first imagined. Consequently, most lose their fear of criminal sanctions at an early age. However, to say the prison experience is "nothing" is probably not true for most lifestyle criminals, particularly as they approach midlife. Typically, as offenders grow older they no longer find penitentiary life as exciting and stimulating as they once did. As a result, they begin to fear the prospect of dying in prison. The fear of dying in prison may actually hold the same deterrent value for lifestyle offenders that fear of criminal sanctions holds for many noncriminals.

Cognitive Indolence

The lifestyle criminal is lazy in thought as well as action. This laziness of thought, referred to by the lifestyle theory as cognitive indolence, sets the stage for relapse. Offenders exhibiting a moderately high degree of cognitive indolence fail to effectively challenge their thinking. This, in turn, allows other features of criminal thinking to take root. Before long, criminals with good initial intentions may find themselves in trouble with the law because they believed they had their problems under control and stopped challenging their thinking.

IND-1: "It's easier to avoid obligations than meet them."

Comment: This demonstrates the nearsighted nature of criminal perception. While it may seem easier to drop out of school, quit one's job, or avoid paying the phone bill, these short-term solutions to life situations will likely result in long-term problems for the individual. The lifestyle criminal will then take even more drastic steps in attempting to solve the problems he or she has created. This might include picking up a gun, looting a store, or burglarizing a home. As with previous attempts at problem solution, such measures will create many more difficulties than they solve.

IND-2: "It'll work out!"

Comment: The lifestyle criminal can be heard telling family and friends that everything will work out, though he or she has no real idea how to pull this off. The goals espoused by the average high-rate offender are frequently lofty and unrealistic. In addition, such persons typically approach long-range goals with a short-range mentality and rapidly become frustrated if their efforts do not lead to immediate results. The lifestyle criminal may therefore benefit from instruction designed to teach problem-solving and goal-setting skills. In the end, the lifestyle offender must learn to establish realistic short-, medium-, and long-range goals and then implement steps to attain them.

IND-3: "Why take the conventional path when shortcuts are available?"

Comment: This statement speaks to the heart of cognitive indolence and demonstrates how resistant the individual is to adopting a conventional approach to life. Many lifestyle criminals prefer taking the shortcut as opposed to the conventional path, even when they know that this shortcut is fraught with long-term difficulties. Cognitive indolence is simply one more way habitual lawbreakers set themselves up for failure.

Discontinuity

The discontinuity of offender thinking is probably the most insidious feature of the criminal lifestyle. Unlike mollification, sentimentality, and superoptimism—which are tied to the content of specific thoughts—discontinuity is a process feature of criminal cognition. For this reason, discontinuity is troublesome to pinpoint and nearly impossible for the offender to identify. Like cognitive indolence, discontinuity interferes with effective problem solving and goal attainment. It also allows the offender to continue to engage in serious criminality without realizing the contradictory nature of some of his or her behaviors. This compartmentalization of experience provides the lifestyle criminal with an avenue through which he or she can resist attempts to bring about a long-range shift in behavior.

Discontinuity is not only the most difficult aspect of criminal thinking for offenders to identify within themselves, but also the most problematic of the eight thinking patterns to modify. Yochelson and Samenow (1976) recommend use of a moral inventory in which the offender jots down his or her thoughts and then discusses them with the counselor or therapy group. This would appear to be a particularly effective tool in the fight against discontinuity since it provides the subject with the opportunity to observe the inconsistent machinations of criminal thought. As is the case with all eight of the thinking patterns discussed here, learning to effectively handle discontinuity is a lifelong process and one that requires continued attention if the individual is to remain free of the legal entanglements that have plagued him or her for so long.

Aspects of the eight thinking patterns of lifestyle criminality can be found in nonlifestyle criminals as well, although not to the same degree. Confronting the resistance displayed by lifestyle criminals during the formative stages of the therapeutic relationship is of paramount significance and requires a counselor who is willing to be both honest and direct.

Honesty and directness are the hallmarks of an effective therapeutic relationship with a lifestyle criminal. Therapeutic interventions with the lifestyle criminal are a two-way exchange in which the counselor solicits information from the offender, shares some of his or her perceptions with the offender, and then introduces the offender to the necessity of taking responsibility for his or her actions. To make the most of limited therapeutic resources, intervention should be educational and behavioral, rather than client-oriented or dynamic, although continued follow-up is essential for long-term success with high rate offenders.

Possibly the most important consideration in managing condition-, choice-, and cognition-based resistance is to avoid entering into an extended debate with the lifestyle criminal. The therapist can point out the self-defeating nature of the individual's behavior and suggest that continuing to engage in such behavior will probably result in imprisonment in the near future. It is not the counselor's job, however, the make the offender's decision for him or her or to recommend which option the offender should select. Rather, the counselor simply provides the lifestyle criminal with information, feedback, and the realization that the choice of whether to continue with criminality or develop a noncriminal lifestyle is entirely up to the individual.

Table 1

The Eight Cognitive Characteristics of Lifestyle Criminality

Characteristic	Reference	Description
Mollification	Walters (1990)	Rationalizing or justifying past criminal action by pointing to societal injustice, the failings of others, or by blaming the victims of one's crimes.
Cutoff	Walters (1990) Yochelson & Samenow (1976)	Rapid elimination of deterrents to criminal action. The cutoff can either be internal or external.
Entitlement	Walters (1990)	Belief that one is entitled to violate the laws of society or the personal rights of others by virtue of ownership, professing their uniqueness, or because they have a habit of misidentifying wants as needs.
Power Orientation	Walters (1990)	The belief that power and personal strength are the goals of life, the absence of power being experienced as a zero state that the individual attempts to overcome by power thrusting (Yochelson and Samenow 1976).
Sentimentality	Walters (1990) Yochelson & Samenow (1976)	Offender will point to the positive things he or she has done and that there is really no need for him or her to change his or her behavior. This is also known as the "Robin Hood Syndrome."

Characteristic	Reference	Description
Superoptimism	Walters (1990) Yochelson & Samenow (1976)	Unrealistic appraisal of one's chances for success in various criminal and noncriminal ventures. Though the lifestyle criminal realizes that there is a chance of getting caught at some point in the future, he or she convinces him or herself that there is no way he or she will be apprehended "this time."
Cognitive Indolence	Walters (1990)	Lazy, noncritical thinking that finds a lifestyle criminal speaking in generalities and avoiding specifics. With cognitive indolence, shortcuts are the preferred means to an end.
Discontinuity	Walters (1990)	Lack of consistency, congruence, or continuity in thinking, which draws the lifestyle criminal to various enticements and temptations present in the surrounding environment.

References

Ball, J. C., J. W. Shaffer, and D. M. Nurco. 1983. The day-to-day criminality of heroin addicts in Baltimore—A study in the continuity of offense rates. *Drug and Alcohol Dependence* 12: 119-142.

Chaiken, J., and M. Chaiken. 1982. *Varieties of criminal behavior*. Santa Monica, Calif.: Rand Corporation.

Figgie Corporation. 1988. *The Figgie report. Part VI: The business of crime*. Richmond, Va.: Figgie International.

Hamparian, D. M., R. Schuster, S. Dinitz, and J. P. Conrad. 1978. *The violent few.* Lexington, Mass.: Lexington/DC Heath.

Kandel, E., S. A. Mednick, L. Kierkegaard-Sorensen, B. Hutchings, J. Rosenberg, and F. Schulsinger. 1988. IQ as a protective factor for subjects at high risk for antisocial behavior. *Journal of Consulting and Clinical Psychology* 56: 224-226.

Kellam, S. G., R. G. Adams, H. C. Brown, and M. E. Ensinger. 1982. The long-term evolution of the family structure of teenage and older mothers. *Journal of Marriage and the Family* 44: 539-554.

Monahan, J. 1973. Abolish the insanity defense?—Not yet. *Rutgers Law Review* 26: 719-740.

Osborn, S. G., and D. J. West. 1980. Do young delinquents really reform? *Journal of Adolescence* 3: 99-114.

Samenow, S. E. 1984. *Inside the criminal mind.* New York: Times Books.

Shannon, L. W. 1982. *Assessing the relationship between adult criminal careers to juvenile careers: A summary.* Washington, D.C.: Office of Juvenile Justice and Delinquency Prevention.

Walters, G. D. 1990. *The criminal lifestyle: Patterns of serious criminal conduct.* Newbury Park, Calif.: Sage.

Walters, G. D., and T. W. White. 1988. Society and lifestyle criminality. *Federal Probation* 52: 52-55.

Walters, G. D., and T. W. White. 1989a. Heredity in crime: Bad genes or bad research? *Criminology* 27: 455-485.

Walters, G. D., and T. W. White. 1989b. The thinking criminal: A cognitive model of lifestyle criminality. *Criminal Justice Research Bulletin.* 4(4).

Werner, E. E., and R. S. Smith. 1977. *Kauai's children come of age.* Honolulu: University of Hawaii Press.

Wolfgang, M., R. F. Figlio, and T. Sellin. 1972. *Delinquency in a birth cohort.* Chicago: University of Chicago Press.

Yochelson, S., and S. E. Samenow. 1976. *The criminal personality: Vol. I. A profile for change.* New York: Aronson.

"Rehabilitating" White Collar Criminals

George A. Harris, Ph.D.

White collar crime is estimated to cost the American economy between 40 and 200 billion dollars annually—five to ten times more than the cost of street crime (Coleman 1985; Boquax 1985). But street crime gathers most of the attention of the public and of law enforcement officials, perhaps because of its immediate effects and often violent nature. White collar crime was first defined by Sutherland (1949), a sociologist, and much of the later study of white collar offenses has been done by sociologists, not psychologists.

Little has been written on what kind of "rehabilitation," if any, would be effective for white collar offenders. Sociologists tend to focus on ways to change the structure of social institutions and legal processes but are less often concerned with therapeutic work with individuals than are psychologists. There seem to be no thorough attempts to conceptualize the rehabilitation of white collar offenders. Smith and Berlin (1988) also note the shortage of sociopsychological theory to guide research on white collar criminals.

At the federal corrections level, white collar offenders may be sentenced to federal penitentiaries or prison camps, but there are no treatment programs specifically designed for such offenders (Walters 1989). State systems also focus largely on street offenders, although white collar offenders are sent to state prisons or to halfway houses to serve sentences.

Thought Processes

There have been articles examining psychological characteristics and thinking processes of white collar offenders. Cressey (1953) studied embezzlers and their use of neutralization techniques to deny responsibility for their acts. Neutralization techniques are aimed at denying that there is a victim, an injury, or personal blame. For example, the embezzler commonly refers to embezzlement as "borrowing," a cognitive strategy to deny loss to the "lender."

It is important to note that neutralization techniques are

necessary only for people whose basic values are social. Offenders who have internalized antisocial values have no need to excuse their behavior to protect self-concept (Green 1990). Furthermore, neutralization is different from rationalization, which *follows* the criminal act. Rationalization is an automatic and unconscious repression designed to deal with guilt (Green 1990).

Sykes and Matza (1957) described five neutralization techniques used by juvenile offenders. The following techniques may also be relevant to white collar offenders:

- denial of victim
- denial of injury
- denial of responsibility
- condemnation of condemners
- appeals to higher loyalties

Minor (1988) adds two more neutralizations: necessity ("I need the proceeds of this crime"); and metaphor of the ledger ("I only do this occasionally").

Smith and Berlin (1988) review three cognitive processes that were used by Watergate criminals to explain their crimes:

- authorization (someone higher up approved)
- routinization (this is just the way it's always done)
- dehumanization (those who were affected by our acts are less important than other people)

Charny (1982) noted essentially the same mental processes in Nazi war criminals and other perpetrators of genocide at various times in history.

Benson (1985) discussed cognitive strategies used specifically by white collar offenders in their efforts to deny guilt, minimize the seriousness of their rule-breaking, and retain a view of themselves as "good" people. Walters (1990) notes that Benson's findings were remarkably similar to those of Yochelson and Samenow (1976), who studied offenders adjudicated not guilty by reason of insanity after committing serious crimes against property and person. Yochelson and Samenow identified fifty-two thinking errors displayed by criminal offenders but were unable to identify social or environmental causes of these thinking errors. Samenow believes that the thinking errors of white collar offenders are the same as thinking errors of street offenders. However, to date there has been no study of this hypothesis.

Walters (1990) summarizes the thinking errors into the following eight categories:

- mollification (blaming others)
- cutoff (mental strategies to avoid thinking about consequences)
- entitlement (belief that one is owed)
- power orientation (use of power to intimidate others)
- sentimentality (doing good deeds to make up for bad deeds)
- superoptimism (extreme confidence that one will not be caught)
- cognitive indolence (always looking for the easy way)
- discontinuity (failure to see inconsistencies between stated values and deeds)

It appears that these various authors are identifying similar thought processes (distortions) in white collar offenders. For example, mollification is essentially the same as the neutralization tactic of condemning the condemner; sentimentality is the equivalent of metaphor of the ledger in that the offender excuses self for illegal acts by adding up offsetting good acts.

Personality Characteristics

There have been efforts to identify personality characteristics of white collar offenders. One would expect that a person who displays certain thinking errors (distortions) would have a recognizable "personality" profile. However, cognition and personality are related though separate concepts. Sutherland (1949) contended that offenders and nonoffenders were not different on various personality measures. Through clinical interviews, Bromberg (1965) concluded that one white collar offender was egocentric, rigid, stubborn, and uncompromising. His subject was said to have an unconscious feeling of omnipotence. In this description, we can see the similarity to the thinking errors of superoptimism and entitlement described earlier. Hirschi and Gottfredson (1987) saw such characteristics as impulsiveness and aggressiveness as related to both street crime and white collar crime.

Coleman (1985) summarized the literature exploring psychological characteristics of white collar offenders, concluding that they were more reckless and aggressive than nonoffending employees. He added, however, that it is the social environment that is the central cause of crime, although it may be the personality differences of individuals that determines who will commit the crimes. Coleman added that various kinds of white collar crimes might be committed by different personalities. For example, nonconformists might be more likely to become involved in crimes against their employer but less likely to go along with organizational crime that their employer demanded.

Some of Yochelson and Samenow's thinking errors, such as power orientation, lead to abuse and violence toward other human beings and therefore seem to reflect an underlying antisocial bent to the offender's personality. Yet as Charny (1982) noted, so-called "normal" personalities are found in those who perpetrate mass murder and genocidal acts around the world and justify such acts by dehumanizing their victims with racist terminology (gooks, niggers, kikes, etc.).

It may well be that white collar offenders have no characteristics currently recognized as psychiatric disorders. Charny proposed the need for a new psychiatric classification to encompass what he believed to be patently obvious: There must be something wrong with those who can dehumanize people sufficiently to kill millions without feeling guilt. Likewise, current diagnostic concepts may be inadequate to distinguish personality disorders in white collar offenders, yet it is clear that some people do tremendous damage to others, financially and physically, through their crimes while others do not commit such crimes given the same opportunity.

Much empirical research is needed before concluding whether personality or thinking errors can be linked to the commission of white collar crimes. But then it is not clear that white collar crime can be neatly explained by societal variables either. For example, Coleman (1985) noted that our capitalistic, materialistic, and competitive society was the clearest cause of white collar crime. However, Smith and Berlin (1988) argued that socialist countries, including the Soviet Union, Cuba, and China, also have serious problems with white collar crimes, suggesting that capitalism is not the sole cause of the problem.

Types of White Collar Crime and Their Treatment

While the social and psychological causes of white collar crime are being debated, white collar offenders are being prosecuted and sentenced to correctional programs where presumably rehabilitation and counseling are being performed. What do we do with such offenders until we have clear conclusions about the causes of their behavior? While recognizing that societal pressures may be causally related to white collar crime, as they are to street crime, therapists nevertheless are asked to provide rehabilitation services.

The research on cognitive processes of offenders suggests that some type of cognitive psychotherapy might be useful in changing criminal behavior. Yochelson and Samenow's methodology of using offenders' daily phenomenological logs of thinking to correct errors is an interesting approach, but other therapists might prefer other techniques. The point is that some conceptualization of white collar offender treatment needs to be developed regardless of whether theorists have agreed on the precise causes of white collar crime. A review of the various types of white collar crime may help to further conceptualize what kind of psychological treatment might be useful and what issues a counselor or therapist would face.

Occupational crime is the commission of a theft by a company's employee. The employer frequently terminates the employee without involving the authorities (Coleman 1985; Coleman 1987). The average citizen generally (1) does not feel directly and personally threatened by this type of crime; (2) does not understand the details or legalities of complicated financial crimes; and (3) does not demand law enforcement action. To the extent that society is not distressed about such crimes, it is easier for occupational offenders to maintain their self-images of noncriminals (Smith and Berlin 1988). Consequently, the correctional counselor may need to break through substantial denial to help the offender take responsibility for the act.

Unlike street criminals, occupational offenders have jobs and are typically middle or upper class. A common goal of rehabilitation for street offenders is to prepare them for jobs. It is sometimes argued that unemployment causes crime. But the goal of finding jobs for white collar criminals makes little sense if they had good jobs while committing their crime. Hirschi and Gottfredson (1987) pointed out that deprivation and other criminological "strain" theories are not persuasive explanations of white collar crime and may not be for street crime either. It seems clear that mere lack of employment is not the cause of white collar crime, and therefore job training will not be a rehabilitative solution.

Organizational white collar crime occurs when a business conspires to defraud the public through false advertising, faulty products, or other deceptions (Coleman 1985; Clinard and

Quinney 1978). Organizational white collar crime can be physically harmful, contrary to the myth that white collar crime is nonviolent. Ralph Nader's ground-breaking investigations detailed in *Unsafe at Any Speed* showed clearly that corporate behavior can create physical danger. The physical damage to people inflicted by dangerous cars, chemical waste, and other unsafe products is enormous, but it is difficult to prove legally that companies and their officials had criminal intent behind their actions (Coleman 1985).

When corporate officials are convicted of crimes, counselors will likely be faced with complex problems of denial by the offender. Such clients may argue that the corporate climate or demands of the marketplace produced such pressure to act illegally that they feel no personal responsibility for carrying out the directiveness of corporate policy. This is the neutralization tactic of authorization, or to use Walters' terminology, mollification.

Such verbal strategies to deny responsibility seem no different in principle from the strategies to deny responsibility used by street offenders. But it is not known whether white collar offenders would learn better in a homogenous group of other white collar offenders or in a heterogeneous group mixing white collar and street offenders. Consequently, it is not clear whether white collar offenders would be better or worse off if sentenced to serve time or participate in group treatment with street offenders in a rehabilitation program. It seems likely that white collar offenders would resist seeing the parallel between their own denial of responsibility and the denial by an offender perceived as lower in status in a heterogeneous group.

Treatment of other offender groups, notably sex offenders and batterers (Yochelson and Samenow 1985), is often done in homogeneous groups. In these groups offenders confront and learn from one another readily as they see themselves mirrored in other group members. But there has not been any research or discussion of the relative merits of heterogeneous versus homogenous groups for white collar offenders or any research comparing group versus individual therapy.

Crimes by government officials and crimes against the government are another type of white collar crime. The motivation for these crimes appears to be an important consideration for designing a correctional response.

When the motivation for a crime is financial, it is referred to as instrumental, whether it was a street or white collar crime.

Expressive crimes have other psychological motivations, such as revenge. Some acts by government officials may be criminal, though there is little or no financial gain. The motivation may appear, at least to some, as patriotic. How would a counselor design a treatment plan for Oliver North? What would the goals of treatment be? How would counseling proceed if Colonel North steadfastly denied any feeling of remorse? Therapists might themselves be unconvinced that Colonel North had committed a criminal act. Consequently, it would be difficult for such therapists to confront North about denying responsibility for his crime.

A final example of white collar crime is crime by professionals, such as doctors and lawyers, made possible by their professional positions. Insurance and Medicare fraud are examples of such crimes. Because professional practices are so increasingly technical, it is often difficult for laymen (and counselors) to discern whether a law has been broken. For example, stockbrokers, who provide account service to customers, are prohibited from "churning" these accounts (i.e., trading excessively to rack up commissions). Likewise, lawyers are ethically bound not to sue frivolously for the sole purpose of generating fees. But it is hard to be sure when stockbrokers and lawyers are churning accounts or filing frivolous claims. As a practical matter for the corrections counselor, these particular examples may not be relevant since civil suits would be filed in case of complaint and offenders would not likely be sentenced to a program or diverted for counseling.

The complexity of white collar crime, whether occupational, organizational, political, or professional, leads to another issue relevant for treatment: Is the offense only an offense because of technical considerations that are related to changing standards? Insider trading (trading on the basis of nonpublic information) may be an example of an action which, at one time, was considered perfectly acceptable by almost everyone. Many stockbrokers and company officials assume they have special information naturally as a result of their positions and therefore they should not be excluded from profiting from such access. But changes in attitudes toward protecting the consumer may have made criminals out of many who previously viewed their practices as ordinary and routine. Such offenders might be especially resistant to assuming any responsibility for their behavior. They may feel angry that the rules were changed in the middle of the game. Treatment teams in such programs would require in-service training to understand these crimes and develop an integrated philosophy regarding these technical offenses.

Correctional Response to the White Collar Offender

The corrections counselor in the current criminal justice system does not see a random sample of white collar offenders. Many crimes are never reported, and there is uneven enforcement and prosecution of those that are (Coleman 1986). Furthermore, occupational offenders are probably more likely than organizational and political offenders to be detected, arrested, tried, convicted, sentenced, and incarcerated. Judges have been reluctant to incarcerate white collar offenders (Smith and Berlin 1988). Prison is seen as a place for street criminals, not the middle class white collar offender who might be in physical danger in prison. White collar offenses are most often economic crimes with economic penalties preferred. The effects of recent changes in federal sentencing guidelines and sentencing guidelines in various states are not yet known but may send more white collar offenders to prison, so it is important to at least consider what a treatment facility should have for effective programming. The following are some broad guidelines:

- a professional staff that is knowledgeable about white collar crime and sufficiently sophisticated to interact therapeutically with offenders whose status is often as high as the counselor's
- a program structure that has a coherent treatment philosophy and services, including psychotherapy, psychoeducational activity (values clarification, training in ethics, philosophy, etc.), community service, and restitution
- an appropriate degree of supervision and control to merit consideration as a correctional program in which offenders are both safe and accounted for
- an evaluation component to report outcomes of services

Such programs could be either public or private and could be run in an institution, a halfway house, or outpatient facility. The programs could be funded by a combination of public funds and user fees. That is, there is no reason why offenders should not pay for services rendered. Such a treatment program could be an attractive alternative to other correctional programs and well worth the cost to offenders if it allowed a less restrictive and safer environment than state or federal prisons.

However, the first step to development of such a program is to outline a treatment program that has theoretical merit and potential for rehabilitative success.

Developing a Treatment Philosophy for White Collar Offenders

Development of any correctional program is difficult because of contrasting philosophies about the causes of crime and methods of responding to offenders. As with street offenders, it could be argued that white collar criminals need punishment, not rehabilitation, or that treatment of the individual does not address the root causes of the problem, which reside in society and not in the individual.

Even though white collar offenders may not have an identifiable psychiatric disorder, it is arguable that the offender must be rationalizing or using some other defense to justify the damage inflicted on others. The sociologist may explain such behavior in terms of environment, group norms, and social pressures, but the psychologist examines mental processes (thinking errors, defense mechanisms, etc.) to explain behavior, and it is not necessary for there to be an identified cause to use such psychological concepts in counseling offenders.

A comprehensive program for the white collar offender should address the whole person: substance abuse problems; marital and family difficulties; and certainly the offender's inevitable pain and stigmatization due to the stress of the adjudication and incarceration process, in addition to the underlying personality characteristics or thought process that led to the crime.

A complete treatment program will proceed from a thorough understanding of the individual, his or her crime, the circumstances that created the opportunity for the crime, and the victim. Modern correctional programs must also respond to the needs of the larger society by cooperating with the legal system that refers the offender for treatment. The effect of legal sanctions and punishment on the behavior of white collar offenders should be evaluated along with the rehabilitation program.

The steps of a treatment program for white collar offenders might look like this:

1. Review of presentence investigation
2. Determination of eligibility for program
3. Completion of an individualized justice plan
4. Completion of a clear contract outlining expectations and responsibilities of program, client, and referral source
5. Restitution agreements, if any
6. Community service agreements
7. Evaluation, diagnosis, and treatment planning with provision for: psychoeducational activities (ethics instruction, values clarification, etc.); individual and/or family therapy; group therapy
8. Delivery of treatment (including supervision and in-service training for staff); development of house rules/therapeutic community

The goals of a treatment program for white collar offenders would not be substantially different from the goals of a treatment program for other offenders:

- reduction of recidivism of offenders
- return of offenders to significant or comparable preincarceration employment
- management of post-trauma stress of adjudication/incarceration
- other individual client goals (drug/alcohol treatment, etc.)
- successful program completion, including restitution and community service

White collar crime represents a greater financial harm to the public than street crime. White collar crime can also cause physical harm. Yet the correctional system has done little to provide "correction" to those offenders who have reached the prison gates and has done less to establish meaningful programs that would encourage the sentencing of such offenders for rehabilitative purposes.

Though cultural forces may set the broad outline of a climate that places acquisition of wealth over the rights and safety of the public, only a small percentage of individuals engages in activity that would be called white collar crime. It is not clear what causes select people to commit white collar crimes, but there is evidence of thought processes that seem to be common to offenders generally. Therapists who understand these thought processes will be better equipped to deal with denial and resistance to treatment.

It is both possible and necessary to develop correctional programs and psychological approaches for working with individual white collar offenders. Incarceration is punishment, and its effects on white collar offenders need to be understood. But psychological treatment within the correctional institution may also be beneficial for both the individual offender and society.

References

Benson, M. 1985. Denying the guilty mind: Accounting for involvement in a white collar crime. *Criminology* 23(4): 583-608.

Boquax, A. 1985. *White collar crime.* Lexington, Mass.: Lexington Books.

Bromberg. 1965. *Crime and mind.* New York: Macmillan.

Charny, I. 1982. *"How can we commit the unthinkable?" Genocide: The human cancer.* Boulder, Col.: Westview Press.

Clinard, M. B., and R. Quinney. 1978. Corporate crime: Issues in research. *Criminology* 16: 255-272.

Coleman, J. 1985. *The criminal elite.* New York: St. Martin's Press.

Coleman, J. 1987. Toward an integrated theory of white collar crime. *American Journal of Sociology* 93(2): 406-439.

Cressey, D. 1953. *Other people's money: A study in the social psychology of embezzlement.* Glencoe, Ill.: Free Press.

Green, G. 1990. *Occupational crime.* Chicago: Nelson-Hall.

Hirschi, T., and M. Gottfredson. 1987. Causes of white collar crime. *Criminology* 25(4): 949-974.

Minor, W. 1981. Techniques of neutralization: A reconceptualization and empirical verification. *Journal of Research in Crime and Delinquency* 18: 295-318.

Nader, R. 1965. *Unsafe at any speed.* New York: Grossman.

Samenow, S. 1988. *Inside the criminal mind.* New York: Time/Life Books.

Smith, A., and L. Berlin. 1988. *Treating the criminal offender, 3rd ed.* New York: Plenum Press.

Sutherland, E. 1949. *White collar crime.* New York: Dryden.

Sykes, G., and D. Matza. 1957. Techniques of neutralization:

A theory of delinquency. *American Sociological Review* 22: 667-670.

Walters, G. 1989. *The criminal lifestyle: Patterns of serious criminal misconduct.* Newbury Park, Calif.: Sage.

Yochelson, L., and S. Samenow. 1976. *The criminal personality. Vol. I: A profile for change.* New York: Jason Aronson.

Yochelson, L., and S. Samenow. 1985. *The criminal personality. Vol. II: The change process,* (revised ed.) New York: Jason Aronson.

Yochelson, L., and S. Samenow. 1986. *The criminal personality. Vol. III: The drug user.* New York: Jason Aronson.

Working with the Resistant Cocaine Abuser

Harry M. Brown, Ph.D.

Working with substance abusers requires treatment approaches and concepts that are different from those applied toward other mental health problems. Though there are commonalities in the treatment process and structure for all substance abusers, it is essential in working with cocaine abusers to understand the unique properties of cocaine and the special techniques that need to be applied in treatment.

Resistance will be encountered in all phases of treatment with cocaine abusers, from the initial difficulties encountered in getting them into counseling to maintaining them in treatment and subsequent aftercare programs. The key to planning treatment techniques through all phases of recovery involves understanding the specific physiological and psychological effects of cocaine and the personality dynamics and behavioral results associated with usage.

Cocaine's Physiological Properties

Though the drug myth of the 1970s and early 1980s portrayed cocaine as a safe, nonaddictive drug, it is now generally recognized as the most powerful reinforcing substance known. In research studies, laboratory animals given unlimited access to cocaine continued to use until they died. In one study, Rhesus monkeys allowed to self-administer cocaine every ten seconds died within five days (Johanson et al. 1976). In another study (Bozarth and Wise 1985), the usage of cocaine vs. heroin in laboratory rats was compared. After thirty days, eleven of the twelve rats given unlimited access to cocaine were dead, while only four of the eleven heroin-using rats died. The rats receiving cocaine lost up to 47 percent of their body weight, stopped grooming, and had rapid deterioration in health. For humans using cocaine, there are countless horror stories regarding the complete deterioration in physical, psychological, and moral behaviors that accompany prolonged usage. Cocaine abusers have been known to sell all of their possessions, including their clothes, to obtain the drug. In Kansas City recently, a woman sold her newborn baby for a $20.00 vial of crack.

The powerfully reinforcing nature of cocaine occurs because of its two primary activating characteristics within the body: it is a central nervous stimulant and also works as a sympathomimetic. As a central nervous system stimulant, cocaine energizes, intensifies and speeds up body systems, causing increases in blood pressure, heart and breathing rates, body temperature, and skeletal-muscle tension. While this stimulation can induce a feeling of well-being, it is cocaine's action as a sympathomimetic that is the primary reinforcing property of the drug. When ingested, cocaine stimulates the release of neurotransmitters such as dopamine and norephinephrine in the brain. These neurotransmitters, which produce feelings of euphoria and pleasure, are then produced at a faster and quantitatively greater rate than normal. In addition, cocaine usage produces a phenomenon not found in non-stimulant usage: it prevents the re-uptake of the neurotransmitter back to the original nerve site. In normal brain functioning, after the neurotransmitter has been sent from one nerve cell to the next, it is pumped back by the original nerve cell. But cocaine fits into the pump site and blocks the re-uptake, thus prolonging an intense feeling of euphoria.

This intense euphoria and the subsequent crashing or dysphoria encourages cocaine users to binge to maintain peak intensity for as long as possible. Binge using becomes an incredibly powerful reinforcing experience that produces future consequences and difficulties for the abuser that can be understood within the domain of classical conditioning principles. Simply stated, classical conditioning principles imply that phenomena connected in time or space with powerful reinforcing stimuli can take on the properties of that stimuli. With cocaine usage there are a number of stimuli that become associated with drug usage and thus develop the power to bring forth cravings and desires within the abuser, as if cocaine were put in front of them.

These stimuli have been labeled as triggers and have been known to create intense desires to use cocaine when encountered by the abuser. Some of the more powerful triggers for cocaine abusers are extra money, drug paraphernalia, physical proximity to dealers or people who abuse, weekends, and the recounting of war stories about "how they use." These triggers have been known to last for months, and this phenomenon is a significant contributor to the high relapse rate demonstrated by cocaine abusers.

Personality Factors

Another contributor to the strong resistances to treatment encountered in working with cocaine abusers involves their personality dynamics. It is not clear whether cocaine usage causes certain personality styles to appear, or whether people with certain personality styles are attracted to cocaine because they like the "rush, power, and intensity" of the drug. It is quite likely that most abusers already have a predisposition toward different personality styles and that cocaine abuse heightens and pushes to the extreme certain personality characteristics. The personality traits most commonly described for cocaine abusers include narcissism, egocentrism, and a need for excitement. Some of the terms treatment personnel use to describe cocaine abusers are grandiose, terminally unique, hyperactive, extremely controlling, domineering, self-centered, insensitive to others, distrustful, and materially oriented. Patients with these personality characteristics are going to demonstrate great difficulty in participating in the treatment processes that make therapy successful. Those common treatment experiences for which cocaine abusers' personality traits interfere include bonding, forming therapeutic alliances, depending on and trusting others, and staying in treatment when uncomfortable feelings occur.

In addition, the unique properties of cocaine that make using such an intense experience tend to hinder the "turning over to others and to one's higher power" processes that occur in 12-step recovery groups. Twelve-step groups rely on the principles of admission, surrender, and acceptance. Substance abusers are more likely to surrender their will and accept the concept of sobriety after a long course of physical, psychological, and spiritual deterioration that results in their hitting bottom. By all accounts, cocaine abusers become addicted and subsequently hit bottom much faster than with any other addictive substance. This fast-acting process would appear to be caused by both the powerful reinforcing nature of cocaine and the expense of the drug. But in hitting bottom so quickly, many cocaine abusers have not experienced the cognitive changes necessary to admit that they are out of control of their lives, and they lack the subsequent need to surrender their will. Working with cocaine abusers in this frame of mind can be compared to trying to reel in a fish without letting it "play out" on the line. There may be so much resistance that the line may snap and the abuser may run away from any efforts to involve him or her in a twelve-step or treatment program.

Treatment Issues

Taking into consideration the various sources of resistance described earlier, it is clearly not an easy task to induce cocaine abuses to enter into or stay in treatment. Similar to any other addiction, cocaine abusers are unlikely to enter treatment unless they are in sufficient pain or unless there is sufficient leverage motivating them to seek help. The disease model of addiction is applicable to cocaine abuse and this model implies that the vast majority of substance abusers do not seek help until the pain and consequences are so great they feel they don't have a choice.

When cocaine abusers have not hit bottom, interventions, as developed by Vernon Johnson (Johnson 1986) of the Johnson Institute, can be very helpful. The more family, friends, and significant others at the workplace who are involved in intervening or pressuring, the better the chance of persuading the abuser to seek help.

Obviously, the more external leverage applied upon abusers, the more likely they will conform to the demands being placed upon them. Pertaining to attempting to get someone into treatment, there can be an advantage in working with the involuntary or legally mandated client. Probation and parole officers who are educated about drug awareness principles can require treatment options as a condition of probation or parole. However, though you can lead the horse to water, you can't really make it drink. Treatment counselors working with cocaine abusers who are forced into counseling need to utilize all their skills and abilities to help the abusers overcome their resentment about being forced into treatment. In overcoming the challenges of helping the legally mandated client internalize the need for treatment, group processes can be of assistance. Because of its power to develop cohesiveness and bonding and because of its potency for confrontation, group therapy for the legally mandated client is an important component of treatment.

Sobriety Issues

Once the cocaine abuser has entered treatment, the goal of treatment is the same as for all substance abusers: sobriety. Sobriety is not only the total abstinence of all addictive chemicals, but a change in attitudes, emotional responsivity, behavior, and lifestyle. Sobriety involves honesty, acceptance, and admission of one's problem, and a lifelong commitment to day-to-day recovery. Because of the personality traits that are prevalent in cocaine abusers, it is quite difficult to get them to commit to complete abstinence. Most cocaine abusers in the early stages of treatment are very resistant to the idea that they have to give up alcohol, pot, and other addictive chemicals. In the early stages of treatment, it is very common to hear the phrases, "I'm not an alcoholic. Why do I have to stop drinking?" or "I can control how much I drink." But it is essential that cocaine abusers stay off all addictive chemicals. Patients who use other drugs after getting off of cocaine either go back on cocaine or become cross-addicted. Use of any addictive substance hinders the recovery of a cocaine abuser as follows:

1. Due to the associative conditioning principle, the use of addictive chemicals can trigger cravings for cocaine. Many cocaine abusers have reported that after drinking alcohol or smoking pot, they wanted the better high that they get from cocaine.
2. Drinking or using drugs puts cocaine abusers in situations with the same playmates or in the same playground. The proximity to other cocaine users can trigger desires to use the drug.
3. When addictive chemicals are taken, will power and judgement are greatly reduced, thus decreasing resistance to the temptation of cocaine.
4. Because cocaine abusers still have the same compulsive personality traits and possibly a biochemical predisposition to substance abuse, cross-addiction is likely to take place, with cocaine abusers switching from one addiction to another.
5. The positive effects of sobriety are diminished, thus making cocaine abusers more susceptible to relapse. Addiction is a shame-based process (Bradshaw 1988) which exacerbates the abuser's feeling of low self-worth and low self-esteem. Sobriety helps to produce increased feelings of self-worth, a greater potential for spirituality, and a greater potential to cope with life's stress in a mature manner.

Using addictive chemicals makes it likely that the abusers will emotionally medicate themselves with the chemical and will ultimately feel bad about themselves when they lose control of usage. Feelings of low self-worth make one much more vulnerable to renewing cocaine usage to produce artificial highs.

Inpatient vs. Outpatient Issues

Once the cocaine abuser has agreed to enter treatment, the counselor is then faced with the decision of whether to refer to an inpatient or an outpatient program. It is the author's preference to place someone in the least restrictive and least expensive treatment option if all other factors are equal. Since there is not sufficient evidence that inpatient programs are more effective than outpatient programs, outpatient treatment programs generally should be considered first (Miller and Hester 1986). There are several indicators that, if present, would make inpatient treatment the preferable initial option. These indicators include the following:

- late stage out-of-control usage
- a lack of stability in the environment
- the presence of serious psychiatric or medical problems
- co-existing abuse of other addictive chemicals

Key Factors in Treating Cocaine Abuse:

There are common treatment elements and principles in the programs established for different kinds of substance abuse. Almost all substance abuse counselors would agree on the importance of sobriety in twelve-step programs and the need for drug information and awareness. But to maximize treatment success in working with cocaine abusers, several principles need to be emphasized.

Minimizing Triggers. Cocaine usage produces incredibly powerful cravings, and numerous stimuli become associated with the desire for cocaine. Whereas, for the most part, recovering alcoholics can be in proximity to alcohol and not crave a drink, this is not true for cocaine abusers who are exposed to cocaine. In the first few months of recovery, it is almost impossible for the cocaine abuser to be exposed to cocaine and not relapse. Additionally, relapse frequently happens when the cocaine abuser has been exposed to a trigger such as carrying around too much money or being around friends who use cocaine.

It is essential that treatment programs take into account the counterproductive effects of triggers and structure individual treatment plans for clients that will protect them from exposure to triggers. Relapses can be prevented by structurally changing the behaviors or plans of the cocaine abuser. This can be done by redirecting clients from paying off their dealers as soon as they get out of treatment, arranging for spouses to pick them up from work when they get their paychecks, and instructing them not to associate with drug-using buddies. While this kind of monitoring and supervision may seem beyond the purview of the normal practitioner, these concrete behavior changes can make the critical difference between sobriety and relapse.

Establishing a Good Therapeutic Alliance. In nonsubstance abuse counseling, establishing a good therapeutic alliance is considered part of the foundation for successful treatment. While this concept has not been ignored in chemical dependency treatment, it does tend to be deemphasized compared to the importance of appropriate substance abuse education and establishment of a recovery program. But in working with cocaine abusers, substance abuse counselors are encountering egocentric, narcissistic personalities who generally do not bond well with counselors, program, or other substance abusers. Without the bonding, cocaine abusers are likely to want to do it "their way," to isolate themselves, or to drop out of treatment early.

Cocaine abusers like to consider themselves unique, and many substance abuse counselors inadvertently alienate cocaine abusers by emphasizing that they are no different from other substance abusers and should not consider themselves special. To promote bonding, strategically it is better for counselors to initially play up to the cocaine abuser's sense of uniqueness, until they have formed a sufficient alliance to maintain treatment. The author has successfully utilized cocaine recovery groups in his outpatient practice and has advocated special cocaine recovery tracks to be utilized within inpatient programs. These tracks offer specialized groups and cocaine education classes, separating cocaine abusers from other substance abusers.

Dealing With Relapse. Preventing relapses has become an essential component to substance abuse treatment (Gorski and Miller 1986). After completion of a structured treatment program, the relapse rate for cocaine abusers is generally considered to be quite high. Over 80 percent of cocaine abusers will have a slip at some point during or after treatment. Substance abuse counselors need to take this high rate of relapse into account to help their clients achieve continued sobriety.

To effectively help cocaine abusers overcome relapse, a

good therapeutic alliance is essential. By maintaining contact—such as calling clients who miss sessions to "check up" on their status—counselors can bring relapsed clients back into treatment. The clients then have the opportunity to learn from their mistakes. Many clients find that what they have learned from the group and counselor after relapse was highly important in helping them achieve long-term sobriety.

For some cocaine abusers, particularly involuntary clients, it can be helpful to have contingency contracts. Contingency contracts should clearly delineate the steps to be followed if usage takes place. For patients who are unable to maintain sobriety, a typical contingency contract could be that the patient will attend 90 Narcotic Anonymous meetings in 90 days or enter an inpatient program. Drug screens, when used with contingency contracts, can be helpful and can counteract the denial processes that occur with relapse.

Working with the family of a cocaine abuser is important to help prevent relapses (Stitz and Roscan 1987). Family dynamics exert considerable influence upon the cocaine abuser, and reducing enabling, caretaking, scapegoating, controlling, and blaming can be effective. In addition, family members are often the ones who are most sensitive to the symptoms that lead to relapse and can provide very useful feedback. Besides Al-Anon, Nar-Anon, and family support groups, family therapy is recommended as part of the basic treatment program for cocaine abusers.

Medication can also contribute to preventing relapse. Antidepressant medication, Bromocriptine, Tegretal, and possibly amino acid combinations, have been shown to be helpful in reducing drug craving. But the prescribing of medication for cocaine abusers should be judiciously considered and closely monitored. Similar to other addicts, most cocaine abusers would love to receive a "magic pill" that would cure them of their addiction. Receiving medication might provide an excuse to not become committed to a recovery program. In recovery, emphasis needs to be placed on sobriety principles, attending recovery meetings, and changing habits and lifestyle. Medication should be considered ancillary to treatment, not the primary focus.

There is one other factor that can be important in preventing relapse. Once the cocaine abuser is involved in treatment and committed to obtaining help, twelve-step recovery groups are extremely important and should be considered a basic element of the abuser's recovery program. While NA would normally be considered the appropriate twelve-step group, I have usually recommended Alcoholics Anonymous (AA) over NA. There are several advantages to recommending AA. In most communities AA has many more meetings and certainly has more available sponsors with long-term (over five years) sobriety. Also in AA, cocaine abusers will not hear the war stories they would hear in NA. Listening to vivid descriptions about how other cocaine abusers got high can stimulate strong cravings in cocaine abusers. Many cocaine abusers have reported getting high after an NA meeting because they were so roused by the stories. Recovery groups led by therapists need to also take this trigger phenomenon into account.

Changing Lifestyles. Middle-to-late stage drug usage typically involves a lifestyle that focuses primarily on using the drug. Cocaine abusers, as previously noted, tend to have a strong need for excitement. By trying to maintain their old lifestyle while giving up the drug, cocaine abusers are setting themselves up for relapse.

To maintain long-term sobriety it is necessary to change attitudes, behaviors, playgrounds, and playmates. If not, the cocaine abuser is likely to put himself back in the same situations that trigger a desire for usage.

Cocaine abusers are attracted to cocaine because they like the intensity of the drug. These are people who like intensity in life and prefer the rollercoaster pattern of extreme highs and lows to stability and serenity. For many coke abusers, sobriety is only possible within the context of moderate lifestyle—learning how to level out and balance life's highs and lows.

The best resource for changing lifestyle patterns is twelve-step groups. AA and NA not only help with sobriety, they teach a whole new way of life that involves responsibility, honesty, and maturity. AA and NA are also highly spiritual programs that can be quite helpful in motivating changes in cocaine abusers, from materialism and excitement to spiritual values and beliefs.

Getting cocaine abusers involved in healthier habits can also be helpful. Exercise can not only help prevent boredom, which the cocaine abuser dislikes, but an active exercise routine may fire up the same neurotransmitters that are involved in cocaine usage. Proper nutrition, stress management techniques, assertiveness training, financial budgeting, and conflict resolution training can all be productive changes in lifestyle.

For the substance abuse counselor, cocaine abusers can be a

difficult population to work with. The powerful reinforcing properties of the drug and the personality traits presented by cocaine abusers create special difficulties for treatment programs that need to be addressed. Utilizing standard substance abuse treatment approaches and principles, the counselor is likely to face strong resistance to treatment. But by taking into account the differences encountered with cocaine abusers, specialized treatment approaches can be used to increase the effectiveness of the treatment program and promote greater opportunity for long-term sobriety.

References

Johanson, C. E., R. L. Balster, and K. Bonese. 1976. Self-administration of psychomotor stimulant drugs: The effects of unlimited access. *Pharmacology Biochemistry Behavior* 4:45-51.

Bozarth, M. A., and R. A. Wise. 1985. Toxicity associated with long-term intravenous heroin and cocaine self-administration in the rat. *JAMA* 254:81-83.

Johnson, Vernon E. 1986. *Intervention.* Minneapolis: Johnson Institute Books.

Bradshaw, John. 1988. *Healing the shame that binds you.* Florida: Health Communications, Inc.

Miller, W. R., and R. K. Hester. 1986. Inpatient alcoholism treatment: Who benefits? *American Psychologist* 41(7): 794-805.

Gorski, Terence T., and Merlene Miller. 1976. *Staying sober.* Independence, Mo.: Herald House.

Spitz, Henry I., and Jeffrey S. Rosecan, (eds.). 1987. *Cocaine abuse: New directions in treatment and research.* New York: Brunner/Mazel.

Counseling the Resistant Chemically Dependent Adolescent

Gregg J. Stockey, M.S., and Daun D. Blain, M.S.

Chemically dependent adolescents can be particularly challenging to the counselor. Often they have been coerced into treatment. As a result they may be reluctant to engage in the counseling process. This manifests itself in many ways, such as missed appointments, tardiness, refusal to give up drugs, refusal to self-disclose, acting out behavior, and other direct and indirect means of resisting behavior change. In this paper the importance of coercion in motivating adolescent chemical dependents to change will be discussed, and practical ways for the counselor to respond to client resistance will be presented. The ideas presented here are relevant and applicable within a wide range of theoretical orientations and counseling models.

The Role Of Coercion

The role of coercion, or motivating involuntary adolescents to participate in therapy for chemical dependency, cannot be overestimated. Because admitting defeat and seeking help are contrary to the aims of adolescence, and chemically dependent adolescents often rebel and reject authority, some coercion may be necessary to initiate treatment. It may be best for the therapist to accept coercion and learn to use it to the client's advantage rather than to bemoan the fact that these clients are not voluntary. The sources of coercion for adolescents to get clean and sober include parents, schools, police, and court systems. One or more of these sources may need to "force" a client into treatment for chemical dependency.

Parents have many ways of coercing youth into treatment, such as threatening hospitalization, withholding cherished privileges such as driving, and constantly pressuring their children to conform to limits. Parents may also threaten non-support (kicking the child out of the home), but this is not recommended except in extreme situations, when other forms of parental leverage have been tried unsuccessfully over a period of time. Judicious use of parental power is an extremely important component of successful substance abuse treatment for adolescents. Counselors can develop skills in helping parents to use leverage, thereby increasing chances for successfully intervening in drug-using behavior. The counselor's ability to join with the parents and empathize with their concerns may be critical to successful initiation of treatment for their minor child.

In recent years, many school systems have wisely moved away from treating substance abuse strictly as a behavior problem. As a result, schools have developed a number of creative approaches to encourage or demand treatment for a student found to be abusing alcohol or illegal drugs. The most common approach seems to be an alternative to a suspension/expulsion program in which students or their parents opt for evaluation, outpatient, or inpatient psychotherapy instead of receiving the typical school consequences. These programs have resulted in earlier and more frequent identification of chemical dependence and have increased the numbers of individuals making themselves available to treatment. Without this type of coercive program, many of these potential clients may drop out of high school with their chemical dependence undiagnosed. Such alternative programs are a necessary and helpful use of coercion, bringing services to those who may not otherwise receive them.

Like school systems, police departments and court systems have begun to look for alternatives to standard punitive consequences for adolescent substance abusers. As a result, they too have coerced youth into treatment, often sparing adolescents serious legal consequences. An example of this type of program is the common DUI school, where perpetrators must attend evaluations and education programs in order to have their driver's licence reinstated. These coercive programs help identify many chemically dependent adolescents whose problems would otherwise go undetected and untreated.

Working With Resistance

Working with substance-abusing adolescents means working with resistance. Whether it is initial resistance to engaging in treatment or resistance further into treatment, the counselor's willingness and ability to work through client resistance will make that counselor more successful. Common counselor counter-transference behavior in addictions counseling includes engaging in power struggles, feeling and acting punitive, enabling, or simply giving up. Being aware of and working through one's own feelings and reactions to these clients in clinical supervision and case consultation is of paramount importance. Understanding the dynamic underpinnings of resistant behavior and intervening with effective strategies are also essential. This premise leads to two important ideas:

1. The thoughts and feelings that underlie resistant behavior vary and fall into several specific domains.
2. The counselor must learn to identify, understand, and intervene accordingly to avoid the pitfalls mentioned.

Any comprehensive alcohol and drug assessment should examine what resistance the client is presenting and the feelings and thoughts at its source. Resistant behavior can take many forms. The feelings and thoughts underneath the resistant behavior fall into the following four general domains:

- simple denial
- fear of failure
- loss of identity
- loss of control

Therefore, the first task is assessing in which domain the resistance lies for any particular client. In the assessment, avoid any initial confrontation of what resistance the client is presenting. The goal is to understand it. This is done by exploring all aspects of the resistance and resistant behavior—keying in on the feelings and thoughts that drive it.

One can take a curious approach, not challenging the person's position. This will come as a welcome change and relief to the resistant client whose experience with family and other professionals has been one of challenging rather than understanding. This approach will help the counselor engage the client and develop a rapport from which to challenge when appropriate. This exploration can take the form of simply asking a series of open-ended questions:

1. What do they consider an alcohol and drug problem to be?
2. How do they fit that description and how do they not fit it?
3. What do they think people have to do to get better?
4. Do they think people have to totally abstain or just attempt to control drinking?

5. Have they ever tried to abstain or control their usage? What happened?
6. How do they feel about attempted change?
7. What fears do they have about change?
8. How do they feel about the struggles they've had with their chemical usage?
9. What would the most difficult part of change be for them?
10. What would life be like without alcohol and drugs?
11. What would it mean to them or about them if they had an alcohol/drug problem?

The answers to the above questions and any other appropriate queries help the professional assess which resistance domain the client is presenting.

Resistance As a Function of Denial

Resistance due to denial is revealed when clients simply do not see themselves as having a problem. Much of initial resistance motivated by denial comes from either lack of accurate information about what addiction is and/or the client not accurately perceiving his or her own chemical usage and/or the consequences of his or her chemical usage by rationalizing, minimizing, etc.

If the source of the resistance stems from a lack of information, then the task is to provide the client with just that—accurate information. This can be done by providing information and handouts during outpatient sessions, assigning readings as "homework" between sessions, suggesting the client attend a workshop or lecture on addictions, or encouraging attendance at an open AA meeting. (You don't have to be addicted to attend open meetings; closed meetings are only for alcoholics.)

If clients have a mistaken impression of their own usage, the task is to help them perceive their usage more accurately. This can be done by requesting collaborative information from family members and employers when appropriate and being exact and specific when asking the following questions:

1. What do they use?
2. How much do they use?
3. How often do they use?
4. What happens when they use?

An essential tool borrowed from inpatient treatment is to have the client write a thorough chemical history and edit it as more information surfaces and defenses fade. Chemical histories should include the time period, drugs used, amounts, frequencies, symptoms of addiction, consequences of usage, and periods of controlled use or abstinence. Again, encourage attendance at AA meetings and ask the client to tell you how well he or she fit in. Another useful technique may be to ask the client to try an "experiment" of either total abstinence or controlled use. If the client is going to try controlled use, have the client pick an amount of time that he or she will agree to not overindulge for an extended period of time (three to six months at the least). A person who genuinely does not have a problem should have no difficulty with this.

Resistance As a Function of Fear of Failure

Resistance due to a pervasive fear that one will not be able to successfully abstain shows itself in a variety of ways. The person often says, "I could quit if I wanted to, I just don't want to." Others who fear failure may quite honestly say, "I'm afraid I can't do it." Others may shift to the use of another mood-altering substance, indicating, "I need something to take the edge off." This fear may also be at the root of statements like, "I just don't want to quit." For clients who fear failure in their recovery, it is essential to provide a sense of security and hope. The therapist must also provide an atmosphere of safety so that clients know they will not be punished if they slip or relapse. Increasing the structure of a client's life and treatment is a way of instilling a sense of security and hope. Reinforcing small successes is also a means toward this end. Counselors can increase the structure in a client's life by doing the following:

- have two or more outpatient sessions per week
- have the person do "90 in 90" (attend an AA or NA meeting every day for 90 days)
- make periodic, brief phone check-ins
- have the person obtain a sponsor and have contact with them every day
- have the person find a home group (one meeting that he or she will attend every week no matter which other meetings are attended to establish a "home" there)

- have the client attend "speaker meetings" where one or two recovering people tell their story and share their experience, strength, and hope

One should also consider the value of short-term hospitalization in the event that the client is unable after several attempts to abstain. Timing is essential so that the client doesn't give up before you suggest inpatient treatment.

Resistance As a Function of Loss of Identity

Many drinkers and substance abusers have made their substance abuse an important part of their identity, and their usage becomes a description of their personalities. Adolescents who refer to self and peers as "burnouts" or "freaks" are classifying people, including themselves, on the basis of drug-using behavior. Asking people to give up their behaviors associated with chemical dependency is equivalent to asking a basketball player to give up basketball or a musician to give up the band. For some teens this is asking them to do something that is quite difficult. A client whose nickname was "Bud," short for Budweiser, comes to mind.

For counselors to successfully work with chemically dependent adolescents they must be empathetic and understanding regarding any loss of identity the client suffers when engaged in treatment. The task is to explore the meaning and significance of chemical use and help clients to replace the loss with other activities that can become components of a self-description or self-image. Alcoholics Anonymous or other 12-Step Programs are invaluable here because members often make AA membership a significant part of their self-image, replacing using peers and using behavior with AA peers and AA activities.

For some adolescent clients who believe that drinking or drugging may be the only thing they do well, the resistance to quitting can be very strong. Sometimes it is possible to buy time with such clients by asking them to give up drinking for a specified length of time without committing to ongoing abstinence. During the abstinence period, explorations of identity issues may lead to increased willingness to identify with other activities. In general, it is helpful to avoid long-term thinking (e.g., "You can't drink forever") and stay with shorter-term outlooks, particularly with highly resistant clients. Some clients may refuse to acknowledge the need for long-term abstinence while agreeing weekly to seven days of abstinence. For many clients it eventually becomes easier to make longer-term commitments. The development of a nonusing identity is a component of this.

Resistance As a Function of Loss of Control

Much resistance to engaging in counseling stems from the loss of control or self-determination evident in being referred for help involuntarily. This is decidedly true for adolescent chemical dependents, most of whom do not have a clear desire to stop using.

It is helpful to attempt developing voluntariness on the part of the client. One way to develop a sense of voluntariness is by using counseling contracts that include goals desired by the client. Contracts can be formal or informal, written or oral, and point a direction for the counseling effort. By allowing clients to influence the content of contracts, their willingness to address issues important to others often increases. If the question "What's in it for me?" has an acceptable answer, voluntariness is more likely.

Although some clients may have initial difficulty in determining what is in it for them to be abstinent, counselors can assist clients in discovering an answer.

For some adolescents, abstinence means an end to getting kicked out of the house, getting arrested, getting suspended or other school consequences, vomiting, and so on. As with any involuntary client, it may be helpful to give away power where appropriate in an attempt to adjust the imbalance of power that is used to coerce an adolescent into treatment. Giving clients the power to influence appointment time and frequency is one way to do this. Also, the counselor can state the obvious, "I can't make you stop using drugs," as a way of acknowledging the client's power in the situation. In each session, counselors can give clients some say in determining topics to be discussed as another way of giving back some power and control. Perhaps most important is the counselor's ability to empathize with a client's resistance to some loss of self-determination. Perhaps restating a situation in which you were coerced into doing something you didn't want to do and discussing your feelings about it can convey to the client that you understand the need to resist.

The Disease Concept and Resistance

Regardless of which domain of resistance is most significant with a particular client, the counselor may find that teaching the disease concept of chemical dependency may assist clients in overcoming their reluctance. The disease concept holds that people develop chemical dependency due to a genetic disposition that is manifested when predisposed people use alcohol or other substances. As with all diseases, the progressive worsening of symptoms is predictable. By pointing out to clients how and where their symptoms fit on the progression of chemical dependency and what symptoms lie ahead if progression is not halted, counselors can sometimes motivate adolescent clients to cooperate voluntarily.

Also, the disease concept implies that being chemically dependent is not the client's fault. It is a genetic predisposition, therefore not of one's doing, but it is the client's responsibility to seek help similar to seeking medical attention for another illness or injury. Identifying oneself as having a disease can be face-saving while simultaneously encouraging a client to accept professional assistance. If a client resists the disease concept, and some will, it may be best to return to the educational moves suggested.

Coercion is often a necessary precipitating factor if adolescent chemical dependents are to receive treatment. Therefore, it is recommended that counselors accept coerced clients into treatment and work cooperatively with parents, schools, and the justice system to assure successful treatment outcomes. Coerced or involuntary chemically dependent clients often resist treatment and challenge the counselor's ability to cope creatively and effectively with the client's resistance. It is helpful to include in an assessment the source of the resistance, which may fall into the domains of (1) denial, (2) fear of failure, (3) loss of control or self-determination, and (4) fear of loss of identity.

Developing a Therapeutic Alliance in the Hospital Treatment of Disturbed Adolescents

Flynn O'Malley, Ph.D.

The concept of the therapeutic alliance has been most widely examined as an aspect of psychoanalysis and psychotherapy (Frieswyk et al. 1986; Greenson 1967; Horwitz 1974; Luborsky 1976). Although the role of the therapeutic alliance in hospital treatment has received little attention in the past, several recent contributions have attempted to clarify the concept (Colson and Coyne 1978; Frieswyk, Colson, and Allen 1984) and to examine its value as an outcome variable in the extended hospital treatment of adult patients (Allen, Deering, Buskirk, and Coyne 1988; Allen, Tarnoff, and Coyne 1985; Colson and Coyne 1978). These investigators have noted that the quality of the therapeutic alliance is a predictor of outcome and is reflected in its appraisal by the members of a multidisciplinary treatment team. Earlier work on the therapeutic alliance focused on the individual relationship between patient and analyst/psychotherapist, although complicated relationship patterns have long been understood to also exist between the hospital patient and the treatment team (e.g., Kernberg 1976; Main 1957; Stanton and Schwartz 1954). In addition, there is ample evidence that qualities of the hospital milieu affect the efficacy of the treatment (Gunderson 1978). It should come as no surprise, then, that in the relationship between patient and treatment team, there is both a general affective/interpersonal ambience and a sense of the degree of the patient's ability and willingness to actively collaborate in hospital treatment.

An examination of the role of the therapeutic alliance in the hospital treatment of disturbed adolescents must take into account the enormous divergence in treatment philosophies, program elements, and administrative structures in various settings. Some programs (especially those that focus primarily or exclusively on group phenomena, as in the "therapeutic community") deemphasize the central role of particular staff members (e.g., the unit director, psychiatrist, or psychotherapist), whereas other programs reflect an attending-physician model in which milieu staff members are primarily charged with containing the patient while the "doctor" does the "real" therapeutic work. Gunderson (1978) argued that outcome is related to three qualities of the therapeutic milieu:

- distribution of responsibilities and decision-making power
- clarity in treatment programs, roles, and leadership
- a high level of staff-patient interaction

This view of a multidisciplinary team working in collaboration, as emphasized by Berlin, Critchley, and Rossman (1984), represents the point of departure for this paper in terms of treatment setting and philosophy.

It may seem curious that the concept of the therapeutic alliance occupies a relatively minor place in the common clinical parlance and literature regarding hospital treatment of disturbed adolescents. In two major works, Masterson (1972) and Rinsley (1980) referred to the therapeutic alliance only with respect to the relationship between the patient and the psychotherapist, not between the patient and the treatment team as a whole. These authors may simply restrict this concept to the sphere of psychotherapy, or they may believe that collaboration in hospital treatment takes place primarily between patient and psychotherapist. It is more likely, however, that adolescent patients in general, and hospitalized adolescents in particular, are most typically viewed (at least in the initial stages of treatment) as being less collaborative and more antagonistic toward treatment than their adult counterparts. Masterson (1972) referred to the initial stage of treatment as the "testing phase" (pp. 109-110), while Rinsley (1980) described this stage as the "resistance phase" (p. 23), both emphasizing the adolescent's tendency to avoid therapeutic collaboration. Adolescent patients who require extended hospitalization or residential treatment often fight against efforts to contain and confront their behavioral dyscontrol, and they avoid exploration of their personal pain and dysfunction because of character pathology, dynamic conflicts, and limitations in ego development. However, in addition to these case-specific aspects, the apparent lack of collaboration may pertain to legal rights or developmental factors.

In light of all these factors, and because of the nature of

adolescent development, I suggest that disturbed adolescent patients seldom begin treatment with any semblance of a therapeutic alliance, and that some fail to develop an optimal alliance even by the end of treatment. Nevertheless, precursors to genuine collaboration can be observed, and attention to these precursors can foster productive involvement in treatment. Some patients are able to progress through early stages to attain a level of genuine collaboration. Thus, by becoming familiar with the obstacles to such collaboration, the precursors to collaboration, and the different levels of true collaboration, treaters can better involve adolescent patients in their own treatment.

Obstacles to Therapeutic Collaboration

In the vast majority of cases, the adolescent inpatient's admission has been empowered by parents or other adults rather than by the adolescent. Pseudomature adolescents may feel that they are losing what few freedoms they have attained; more overtly dependent adolescents feel the trauma of a forced separation from their parents. As Weiner (1970) pointed out, "The adolescent has neither the naivete of the child nor the options of the adult" (p. 354). Adolescent patients (despite some awareness of their need for hospitalization) quite poignantly experience a forced hospitalization as a validation of their internal sense of powerlessness.

In addition to resistances to treatment that are rooted in psychopathology, hospitalized adolescents have normal developmental resistances. Two classic papers focus on the developmental dilemma of the normal adolescent. Anna Freud (1958) described the adolescent turmoil inherent in the attempt to defend against infantile object ties. Blos (1967) portrayed adolescent individuation as a process of disengagement from internalized objects. Both authors emphasized the "regressive pull" toward passivity, dependency, and resurgence in libidinal attachment to parental objects, focusing on the various defensive maneuvers and developmental accomplishments that adolescents employ to combat this tendency. Although recent contributions (Kaplan 1980; Offer and Offer 1975) have significantly modified these views, the intensity of the struggle against regression and its disorganizing and frightening effect as described by Blos and Freud is certainly characteristic of more vulnerable adolescents who require frequent hospitalization.

A primary task of adolescence is the development of a sense of growing autonomy and independence while maintaining connectedness to parental objects. This ability is severely compromised in disturbed adolescents due to deficits in ego development and self- and object-relations, problems in self-esteem maintenance, and intrapsychic and external conflicts. Hospitalization becomes necessary because of the behavioral dyscontrol associated with (1) the rebellious stance of the pseudoindependent adolescent who has forced an early disengagement, (2) the anxiety and despair of the more symbiotic adolescent who feels unable to broach any real separation, and (3) the panic of regressive experiences endured by the psychotically vulnerable adolescent. In any case, hospitalization initially increases the youngster's experience of self as passive, dependent, and powerless. These ego-alien aspects of self are then externalized as resulting from the hospitalization.

Thus there are three distinct sources of resistance to forming an alliance with the treatment team:

- the adolescent's perception that hospitalization is coercive because it is empowered by adults
- the normal adolescent revulsion against passivity and dependence
- the psychopathology of the disturbed adolescent which heightens the reaction to separation from parents and containment in the hospital

During hospitalization, the patient and the treatment team often experience treatment as being "done to" the patient rather than as a collaborative effort. Nevertheless, follow-up research indicates that many adolescents establish a strong sense of relatedness to the treatment team and respond positively to hospital treatment. In fact, treatment inevitably goes well when cooperation and collaboration are ultimately elicited from the adolescent patient. My experience as director of an inpatient psychiatric unit for extended treatment of disturbed adolescents indicates that the therapeutic alliance begins with rudimentary, and often quite disguised, aspects of cooperation. These "precursors" to genuine collaboration can be facilitated or impeded by the actions of the hospital treatment team.

Precursors to Collaboration

Frieswyk et al. (1984) defined the therapeutic alliance in terms of "the patient's collaborative activity" (p. 463). Extending the concept to hospital treatment, Allen et al. (1985)

defined collaboration as "the extent to which the patient *actively* uses the treatment process as a resource for constructive change" (p. 188, italics added). Collaboration involves active participation in treatment and, for purposes of this paper, can be distinguished from its precursors by adding the following: *Collaboration involves the patient's recognition of his or her own contribution to problem maintenance and problem resolution.*

In his delineation of transference and alliance concepts, Adler (1985) argued that:

> *The therapeutic alliance in its mature, stable form is . . . usually only present in a later stage of treatment, although precursors or unstable forms of it may be visible earlier . . . A sequence occurs in the successful therapy of primitive patients: (1) The establishment of stable self-object transferences that sustain them, (2) the increasing capacity to appreciate the therapist as a real and separate person, and (3) the gradual ability to ally themselves with the therapist in the service of accomplishing work. (pp. 115-116)*

The initial expressions of precollaborative behavior by disturbed adolescents in the hospital are similarly based on positive self-object and dyadic transferences. These expressions often occur in relationship to the entire treatment team or unit, not just an individual treater. Many adolescents progress from rudimentary levels of collaboration to more truly collaborative engagement.

By definition, precursors to collaboration do not involve the patient's active participation for the purpose of change, or acknowledgement of a personal contribution to problems, but they do reflect beginning (and often unconscious) aspects of cooperation and engagement. The following collaborative moves are listed hierarchically, beginning with the most rudimentary, but they are not "stages" of precollaboration in the sense that they represent a clear progression from one to the next: (1) acceptance of containment, (2) formation of attachments, (3) communication of symptoms, (4) collaboration in conflict-free spheres, and (5) developmental achievement.

Acceptance of Containment

Some patients demonstrate the most tentative beginnings of cooperation with the treatment team by simply accepting the containment of the hospital setting. Although these patients overtly rail against the containment and the structure, their rebellion is not severe enough to create a permanent sense of alienation from the treatment team or to result in their removal from the hospital environment (as might be the case with an elopement or a damaging assault).

Brad, a 16-year-old, powerfully-built, aggressive young man, was brought to the hospital in handcuffs by police officers. He vowed to kill his frightened parents and asserted that the hospital would be unable to contain him. The treatment team gained some leverage through the patient's probation officer, who clearly informed him that if he left the hospital, he would be arrested and returned to court to face the charges against him. The patient's anger continued sporadically throughout his hospitalization. At first he was threatening and intimidating, but he attacked no one and did not attempt to elope. His threats became less frequent in later stages of treatment. He initially stated that he would remain in the hospital no longer than two weeks. He later modified his position to two months, then six months, and so on.

Containment and structure work best when they are established without ambiguity or ambivalence. Patients such as Brad also need protection from humiliation when they fail to carry out their threats and instead allow containment to continue. Those staff members and other patients who may have felt threatened and intimidated may understandably wish to point out how the patient has "given in," but such a reaction only erodes the patient's self-esteem and impedes cooperation. A more productive response is to regard the patient's compliance as "good judgement."

For patients to establish a sense of relatedness and to develop trust in the effectiveness of hospitalization, they must become convinced that their developmental needs will be met by staff members, who will provide containment, structure, and acceptance of dependency without becoming invested in control for its own sake. Because most adolescent patients externalize their experiences of dependency and passivity, they are hypersensitive to indications that treaters are overly invested in "showing the patient who is in control" or in keeping the patient dependent. An attitude that conveys the treater's interest in the patient's ultimate autonomous functioning in the context of supportive relationships can minimize, or at least avoid contributing to, the patient's perception that "you're treating me like a baby."

Formation of Attachments

Adolescents require relationships outside the nuclear family constellation to fulfill their developmental needs. Normal adolescents begin to loosen their internal identifications from parental objects and to invest themselves in identificatory experiences with other adults and peers. Disturbed adolescents in hospital treatment relate to various members of the treatment team through transferences and projections on the one hand, and through developmental needs on the other. Even the most disturbed adolescent makes some effort to engage in normal developmental activity. This effort may include seeking admiration for accomplishments, asking for help with developmental tasks (e.g., homework), debating social issues, competing in skill areas, and inquiring about staff members' interests or views. A disturbed adolescent's engagement in normal developmental activity with members of the treatment team signals the beginning of tentative collaboration.

Jay, a 14-year-old boy, was admitted to hospital treatment following a period of social withdrawal, stealing, and escalating hostility toward all authority figures in his life. He refused to actively participate in any aspect of his treatment planning, and he required repeated interventions because of his behavioral disruption and verbal abuse of staff members. He learned that one staff member shared his interest in motorcycles, and he began to taunt and tease that staff member about their differing opinions on the quality of various motorcycles. This behavior was seen as the beginning of engagement.

Some staff members might want Jay to stop talking about motorcycles and instead discuss his problems, but imposing such restrictions could impede treatment. This patient saw no reason to discuss his conflicts until he could be sure that his developmental needs would be respected. Thus, although team members should continue their efforts to discuss problems with recalcitrant patients, they should also demonstrate a willingness to discuss some shared interest that might serve as a building block for later collaboration.

Communication of Symptoms

Authorities have long recognized that psychiatric symptoms can serve multiple purposes (Fenichel 1945). At least two are evident in the alloplastic behavioral symptoms of adolescents: (1) to prevent or decrease anxiety, depression, or other dysphoric effects; and (2) to reenact traumatic situations or problematic adaptations to learn how to master them. The adolescent patient's ability to produce and reveal manageable symptom patterns to the treatment team can indicate the beginning of collaboration.

Karla, a 16-year-old young woman with a long history of troubled and self-victimizing relationships with men, vowed at the beginning of her treatment to have no boyfriends during her hospitalization. During the latter half of her hospital stay, she formed a romantic attachment to a male patient on the unit. The young man lacked the sadistic streak of some of her prior choices, and the couple began to engage in controversy with the unit staff, who disapproved of their involvement with each other. Although members of the treatment team were somewhat disconcerted by this situation, it gave them opportunities to explore with the patient the nature of her relationships with men, and it gave her a chance to practice new ways of relating.

Some of Karla's interest in a boyfriend may have served to diffuse her dysphoric anxiety and her feeling of being unwanted, but her ability to collaborate regarding a conflict-laden sphere of functioning had obviously increased. The presence or absence of observable symptoms cannot, of course, be viewed as a unidimensional measure of collaborative beginning. Some patients have so little ego strength and control over symptom patterns that they cannot avoid revealing this behavior. Their dyscontrol pervades the clinical picture and interferes with collaborative work. It is the task of the treatment team to encourage such patients to *limit* symptomatic behavior. However, adolescent patients generally experience less alienation from the treatment team when their symptom patterns are viewed as opportunities for work rather than as disruptions in treatment.

Collaboration in Conflict-free spheres

Some adolescents who resist direct, active collaboration in problematic areas may nonetheless begin to express a willingness to work with team members toward success and mastery in conflict-free spheres.

Nick, a 16-year-old young man with a history of seriously disturbed family relationships, transient episodes of rage, and paranoid thinking, could not accept any view of his hospitalization that defined him as needing help. He defended against his fear of psychosis and protected his fragile self-esteem by expressing disdain of his treatment and treaters. He was, however, interested in playing the guitar, and he could not ignore the obvious expertise of one child care worker and a few other patients. His feelings of competence and control were not threatened by allowing others to help him develop a sense of mastery in this area.

When exceptionally resistant and recalcitrant patients can

begin to experience achievement in nonconflictual areas of functioning, it gives them "good feelings" about their treaters that can gradually lead them to work on more conflict-laden aspects of their lives.

Developmental Achievement

The intense structure and support of hospital treatment can elicit adaptive responses from vulnerable patients whose functioning would collapse in a less supportive environment. In a well-designed and well-functioning hospital unit, the consequences of one's behavior are much easier to predict, and the constant attention of staff members and peers ameliorates the patient's experience of isolation and abandonment. This sense of security provides the patient with energy and confidence to engage in developmental activities that previously were too difficult.

During the initial stages of treatment, Rick disparaged his treaters and disdained treatment. He was negative and pessimistic about any future for himself. He had been removed from several schools for his obstructionistic and aggressive behavior. Although he continued to express negative opinions on the unit, he began to achieve scholastically, started attending public school, and began to work toward a vocation.

School was truly a conflict area for Rick. He did not "collaborate" in his treatment by acknowledging a problem and working on it, but he was able to achieve in that sphere because he accepted the support of his therapeutic environment.

Summary

Most of these examples represent what might be called "precollaborative behavior." In fact, some patients never progress beyond these "precursor" stages, yet nonetheless benefit from their hospital experience. One might argue that the degree to which patients engage the healthy environment of the hospital unit will measurably improve their ego development and the quality of their object relations. It will also substantially reduce their alienation from self and others, increasing the likelihood that they will return to a more normal developmental track. Other patients, however, can engage in more active collaboration.

Collaboration

As distinct from its precursors, collaboration involves both the active use of treatment for constructive change and the recognition of one's own contribution to problems. The definition of collaboration comprises a continuum of possible activities and attitudes ranging from patients' acknowledgment that they can have an effect on their problems to a real exploration of self in collaboration with treaters. In the former scenario, patients work to alter an external situation. In the latter, patients work to achieve personal change by accepting some degree of responsibility for their situation.

Improvement of External Circumstances

Adolescent patients who have achieved some level of engagement with the treatment team and who have become invested in their treatment program can begin to recognize their own contribution to difficulties at school or in family relationships. Although they may initially blame teachers and parents for their dysfunction, they often can gradually acknowledge their own role.

Lisa, a 16-year-old young woman with long-standing feelings of resentment toward her father, could express her hostility toward him only through verbal explosions that left her feeling even more alienated and less competent because her father viewed her outbursts as "ridiculous." Through discussions with treatment team members, Lisa began to recognize that her style of communication with her father relegated her to an infantilized position. She then prepared herself for an encounter with her father in which she could calmly and firmly express her specific dissatisfactions with his treatment of her, yet not attack him so vehemently that he would be unable to reflect on her message.

This case illustrates a level of collaboration in which the patient recognizes her contribution to a problem and takes some responsibility for its resolution. This type of work does not, however, involve any recognition that one's problems are aspects of self that are carried into any environment and that therefore require self-examination.

Self-improvement

Self-esteem is even less stable in the disturbed adolescent than in the normal adolescent. Such patients must therefore build up a significant degree of trust before they can engage in collaborative self-appraisal.

Cal, a 16-year-old schizophrenic young man, was acutely aware of his history of traveling from one institution to another. As his relationships in the hospital unit began to feel supportive and nur-

turing, he began to express a wish to adjust to life outside institutions. He was able to reflect on his experiences of becoming disorganized whenever he was subjected to external stress. He recognized his vulnerabilities, the usefulness of medication, and the necessity for a gradual return to community-based activities.

The type of collaboration illustrated here usually reflects a sense of engagement with the treatment team in which the patient feels a deep level of acceptance and a sense of being valued regardless of personal limitations or liabilities.

Exploration of the Internal Self

Some adolescent inpatients who have progressed well during the initial stages of hospital treatment are able to collaboratively examine aspects of themselves at considerable depth and with extraordinary clarity.

Sid, a 16-year-old young man who was desperately striving for a sense of identity separate from his parents, responded to their visits by engaging in verbal battles over minor issues of control—for example, whether or not he wore an earring. In discussions with treatment team members, the patient readily acknowledged that he enjoyed inflaming his parents and felt powerful after such encounters, yet he was also plagued by feelings of guilt, abandonment, and depression. At one point during the treatment, the patient's parents went on a vacation by themselves, resulting in an extended period between their visits to him. During this time, Sid began to reflect on how powerless and alone he felt, and he recognized the level of his attachment to his parents and how fearful he was of ultimately leaving home.

Such insightful revelations can sometimes have an apparently brief effect on patients; their attitudes may vacillate and they may even demean the insightful experience. At other times, such experiences can be the cornerstone for significant and sustained change.

The therapeutic alliance in psychoanalysis and intensive psychotherapy is a concept related to, but by no means identical with, the disturbed adolescent's collaborative activities in intensive hospital treatment. To say that such patients have established a "therapeutic alliance" belies the realities of adolescent development, the legal and social aspects of the disturbed adolescent's hospitalization, and the gradual and tenuous nature of such collaborative work. Nevertheless, there are levels of collaborative behavior that, if recognized and fostered by the treatment team, can facilitate the treatment of these patients.

Moreover, the course of hospital treatment never runs smoothly from one level of collaborative activity to another. Just as disturbed adolescents may periodically go forward into higher levels of functioning while still struggling with earlier developmental issues, so does their collaborative ability periodically spurt forward only to retreat and then to possibly move forward again. Despite the unpredictability of adolescents' collaborative ability, the treatment team may enhance its effectiveness by advancing its knowledge of conceptual landmarks for judging aspects of collaboration.

References

Adler, G. 1985. *Borderline psychopathology and its treatment.* New York: Aronson.

Allen, J. G., C. D. Deering, J. R. Buskirk, and L. Coyne. 1988. Assessment of therapeutic alliances in the psychiatric hospital milieu. *Psychiatry* 51: 291-299.

Allen, J. G., G. Tarnoff, and L. Coyne. 1985. Therapeutic alliance and long-term hospital treatment outcome. *Comprehensive Psychiatry* 26: 187-194.

Berlin, I. N., D. L. Critchley, and P. G. Rossman. 1984. Current concepts in milieu treatment of seriously disturbed children and adolescents. *Psychotherapy* 21: 118-131.

Blos, P. 1967. The second individuation process of adolescence. *Psychoanalytic Study of the Child* 22: 162-186.

Colson, D. B., and L. Coyne. 1978. Variation in staff thinking on a psychiatric unit: Implications for team functioning. *Bulletin of the Menninger Clinic* 42: 414-422.

Fenichel, O. 1945. *The psychoanalytic theory of neurosis.* New York: Norton.

Freud, A. 1958. Adolescence. *Psychoanalytic Study of the Child* 13: 255-278.

Frieswyk, S. H., J. G. Allen, D. B. Colson, L. Coyne, G. O. Gabbard, L. Horwitz, and G. Newsom. 1986. Therapeutic alliance: Its place as a process and outcome variable in dynamic psychotherapy research. *Journal of Consulting and Clinical Psychology* 54: 32-38.

Frieswyk, S. H., D. B. Colson, and J. G. Allen. 1984. Conceptualizing the therapeutic alliance from a psychoanalytic perspective. *Psychotherapy* 21: 460-464.

Greenson, R. R. 1967. *The technique and practice of psychoanalysis*. New York: International Universities Press.

Gunderson, J. G. 1978. Defining the therapeutic processes in psychiatric milieus. *Psychiatry* 41: 327-335.

Horwitz, L. 1974. *Clinical prediction in psychotherapy*. New York: Aronson.

Kaplan, E. H. 1980. Adolescents, age fifteen to eighteen: A psychoanalytic developmental view. In S. I. Greenspan and G. H. Pollock (eds.), *The course of life: Psychoanalytic contributions toward understanding personality development, Vol. II. Latency, adolescence, and youth* (pp. 373-396). Adelphi, Md.: National Institute of Mental Health.

Kernberg, O. F. 1976. Toward an integrative theory of hospital treatment. In *Object-relations theory and clinical psychoanalysis* (pp. 241-275). New York: Aronson.

Luborsky, L. 1976. Helping alliances in psychotherapy. In J. L. Claghorn (ed.), *Successful psychotherapy* (pp. 92-116). New York: Brunner/Mazel.

Main, T. F. 1957. The ailment. *British Journal of Medical Psychology* 30: 129-145.

Masterson, J. F. 1972. *Treatment of the borderline adolescent: A developmental approach*. New York: Wiley.

Offer, D., and J. Offer. 1975. Three developmental routes through normal male adolescence. *Adolescent Psychiatry* 4: 121-141.

Rinsley, D. B. 1980. *Treatment of the severely disturbed adolescent*. New York: Aronson.

Stanton, A. H., and M. S. Schwartz. 1954. *The mental hospital: A study of institutional participation in psychiatric wellness and treatment*. New York: Basic Books.

Weiner, I. B. 1970. *Psychological disturbance in adolescence*. New York: Wiley.

Reprinted with permission from the Bulletin of the Menninger Clinic *Vol. 54, No. 1, pp. 13-24. Copyright 1990, The Menninger Foundation.*

Intervention Strategies for Sexual Abuse

Robert Rencken

Treating the sex offender is a lot like scaling a snow-covered volcano:

- At first, the task seems impossible and one wonders why anyone would undertake it.
- Early discouragement is almost predictable.
- Two steps forward are frequently accompanied by slipping backwards.
- Obstacles are buried and may require a quick change of plans.
- The depth of the snow varies.
- Climbing is best done in teams, with experienced climbers.
- The atmosphere may remain bitter cold or there may be an early thaw.
- Most onlookers are rooting for the mountain.
- *And*, the whole thing may blow up at any time, with or without warning.

Of course, there is some reward at reaching the summit, or coming close to it. Most of the time, however, the counselor needs to gain satisfaction from simply making the journey. This chapter will focus on the segments of that journey, from assessment and crisis intervention to empowerment and risk reduction. The major focus will be on the regressed offender because that profile is encountered most frequently. Specific modifications will be noted for other dynamics.

The offender is probably going to be the only family member mandated for treatment. Although juvenile court may order the child(ren) into counseling, there are typically little or no consequences for failure to comply. On the other hand, the offender risks revocation of probation and incarceration for failure to attend counseling.

Most counselors utilize the concepts of voluntary treatment and confidentiality. Both of these concepts are limited in dealing with pedosexual issues. The offender should be clearly informed of these limitations at the beginning of treatment:

1. Attendance will be reported.
2. Progress and problems will be reported to the treatment team.
3. Violations of probation conditions or court orders will be reported.
4. Financial status (payment of fees) will be reported.
5. Any new allegations of abuse will be reported.
6. The protection of the child will *always* be the primary consideration.

In some cases, the client will have been advised by an attorney not to discuss details of an allegation until after sentencing or plea bargaining. This can be respected through the use of "hypothetical" or general discussions. Counselors will, of course, have to be aware of their own state laws regarding confidentiality or privileged communication. In some cases in local treatment programs agreement may be reached with law enforcement or prosecutors for special confidentiality. The counselor may also have to ensure that the client is represented by an attorney.

How can the counselor establish trust and rapport with these kinds of limitations? The counselor actually may perceive these as an obstacle more so than the client. The client is typically *in crisis* (pain, guilt, anxious about legal system) and in need of support, care, and information. Even the mandatory treatment becomes less of an issue as the clients become "hooked" into treatment. The clients typically grow to see the counselor as the advocate despite these limitations.

The counselor will also need to determine whether treatment (or assessment) will be isolated or integrated. Isolated treatment involves only the offender. In this situation, there may be no plans for reunification of the family or the offense may be extrafamilial. Integrated treatment includes other family members in the treatment plan, regardless of plans for reunification. Integrated treatment is almost always preferred because it builds a support system, increases the effectiveness of taking responsibility, and improves control. However, isolated *as well as* integrated therapy may occur at the same time. The offender will, no doubt, have individual issues to resolve other than the abusive behavior and how it affects the victim. The independent issues may not be appropriate for discussion within the context of family treatment. The need or possibility of this, of course, will be partially determined by the time element.

As quickly as possible, the counselor should determine whether treatment will be short- or long-term. This will depend on:

- *Incarceration.* Only a few weeks may be available until the offender goes to prison.
- *Voluntary treatment.* If there are no legal consequences, the offender and family may terminate treatment early.
- *Divorce.* If there is an early decision to divorce (and relocation of children is involved), the isolated treatment plan might be somewhat shorter.
- *Limited mandated treatment.* It is possible that the courts or CPS may order a prescribed number of sessions or time duration for treatment. It is typically unlikely that families will voluntarily continue after that time.

If it seems that short-term treatment is likely, the focus needs to be on responsibility, impact on the victim, and risk reduction. There should be heavy emphasis on cognitive/behavioral approaches rather than insight/historical approaches.

Assessment/Evaluation

The counselor may be involved in three types of assessment processes:

- *Formal/consultation.* This is a one-time or time-limited process with a goal of recommendations of various types. The counselor generally acts as a consultant in that there is no expectation of ongoing treatment with that counselor/client relationship. The types of recommendations will be discussed later.
- *Formal/ongoing.* The counselor may be asked to do part or all of a formal assessment of a client who will continue in ongoing treatment.
- *Informal/ongoing.* The counselor will be expected to provide ongoing assessment of a client in treatment. This may include diagnosis, prognosis, and treatment plan modification.

Goals of Assessment

Any of these types of assessment may be used with a variety of goals in mind:

- *Evidentiary.* Although there may be some ethical questions involved in this process, the counselor may be asked to help determine whether the accused committed the offense, what happened, and how often. As an alternative, the counselor may be asked if the accused fits the "profile" of an offender.
- *Risk assessment.* The counselor may be asked to determine various kinds of general and specific risk factors. These include the risk of a repeat offense; abuse or threat to children; violence or danger to society; suicide; or probation violation.
- *Rehabilitation potential.* A somewhat different question is whether the offender has a good potential to change his behavioral problems. This includes the potential benefit from treatment or incarceration. It may include an analysis of the offender's resources, both internal (intelligence, personality, health) and external (friends, family, career).

The counselor should know who the client is in these consultation assessments and communicate that clearly to the accused/offender. The client may be the defense or prosecuting attorney, the court (judge), probation department, CPS, juvenile court, or the offender himself. Although the assessment will be objective regardless of the client, the information may be used differently.

Assessment for Treatment Planning

The goals might be different if the assessment is part of a treatment planning process rather than an isolated evaluation. The primary positive factor is the stability and trust inherent in the counseling relationship. Counseling presents a much better atmosphere for supportive confrontation than does an evaluation, particularly regarding responsibility issues. The offender can discuss details of the abuse and the antecedents to it without the pressure implicit in a formal evaluation.

The goals for treatment planning are interactive between the needs of the offender and the victim. If treatment is isolated, without the direct involvement of the victim, consideration can still be given to the actual and potential victim(s).

Goals should be broad enough to address concerns beyond the abuse issues to general self-control, responsibility, and self-esteem.

These latter general issues are extremely important for the treatment planning process. There is a danger that treatment goals may be defined too narrowly, focusing only on the sexual offense and "assurance" of no repeated offense. Although these narrow issues certainly need to be thoroughly resolved, treatment of the more general issues may be an even better predictor of overall adjustment, stability, and control, thereby lowering risk factors. Early in the treatment process, many offenders will claim that they have "learned their lesson" and "will not do it again." Even though they may be correct, they will feel much more confident, and be able to provide more specificity, when the more general issues are resolved.

Assessment Techniques

Clinical Interview

Despite cautions that will be discussed later, the clinical interview is central to any assessment. The key factor, of course, is the judgement of an experienced interviewer. The interview should go beyond the typical mental status examination to include family, social, career, developmental, substance abuse, affective, and responsibility issues.

Family information should include family of origin, current family, and past marriages and families. Significant relationships that did not result in marriage should also be noted. Patterns in relationships should be probed, especially dependency and control issues. The relationship of the subject to each of the children should be supplemented by an understanding of each child's role in the family and family communication patterns.

The focus on social adjustment should include peer relationships (past and current), general relationships with women, isolative tendencies, and leisure activities. Social relationships with children should be probed, such as preference for child-oriented activities, leadership in child and youth groups/teams, or, at the other extreme, abusive hostility toward children.

Although specific careers may not be predictive of a sex offense, there may be a tendency for offenders to choose isolative or dependent job settings. Employment stability and relationships with employers and other employees should be noted.

A developmental history should include physical, cognitive, and intellectual development. A brief medical and educational history should focus on perceived areas of strengths, weaknesses, and specifically, disability or potential rejection.

Patterns of substance use/abuse are a concern not only because of addictive behavior but also as evidence of chronic or crisis-oriented dependency. Denial and minimization should be expected and confronted, particularly among "just beer" drinkers.

Affective awareness is a critical area. Many offenders are particularly unaware of or unable to express feelings. This extends not only to relationship feelings—love, anger, resentment—but to more general feelings like sadness, frustration, and anxiety. An "affective history" should gather data on feelings throughout childhood, adolescence, and adulthood, particularly regarding patterns of affection, nurturance, and dependence.

Finally, responsibility issues should be clarified as much as possible. Ideally, the offender should be able to accept fully the responsibility for his actions. At the time of assessment, however, even those with positive prognoses may not be clearly aware of responsibility early in treatment or may be under legal obligation not to admit liability. In other words, whereas clear acceptance of responsibility is a positive predictor, the absence of it may not be a negative one.

Sex History

A structured sex history should be done separately from the clinical interview. The separation between the two helps in maintaining a systematic approach to the sex history. The history should clearly include all sexual behavior and arousal patterns, with a special focus on early sexual experiences with peers and adults. These childhood experiences should not be labeled as "molestations" or "abuse" by the interviewer in order to circumvent typical denial patterns. Fantasy patterns should be probed in a similar way because initial responses will probably be superficial and minimal.

Psychometric Evaluation

There is considerable disagreement about the efficacy of psychometrics. Part of the problem is in the classification of offenders. MMPI (Minnesota Multiphasic Personality Inventory) profiles that may apply to rapists, for example, will generally not be valid for most pedosexual offenders. The MMPI may, however, be helpful in developing a general diagnostic picture and also may be helpful as a cross-check for credibility and openness versus guardedness. The Multiphasic Sex Inventory

(MSI) may be helpful in a similar manner, as a validation of the sex history. The Millon Clinical Multiaxial Inventory (MCMI-II) may be useful as an alternate or supplement to the MMPI. Projective measures may be helpful depending on the evaluator's experience, but may be more difficult to defend within the judicial system. An intellectual/cognitive measure (e.g., Wechsler Adult Intelligence Scale—WAIS-R) may be needed only if there is some question regarding ability to effectively gain from verbal therapy modalities.

Psychophysiological Measures

Perhaps the most innovative work in the area of assessment has come in the form of psychophysiological measures—the penile plethysmograph and the polygraph. Although neither of these have yet been ruled as admissible evidence in court, they can provide helpful techniques in penetrating the barriers of denial and minimization (Avel and Becker 1984; McGovern and Peters 1988).

The plethysmograph provides a visual readout (graph or digital) of penile arousal through a transducer attached to the penis. Arousal is then measured while the subject is exposed to various stimuli—audio and visual tapes, slides, or films with various themes, both normal and "deviant," including children, nudity, rape, or seduction. Patterns of arousal are noted and explored with the subject, either while on or off the plethysmograph.

The polygraph ("lie detector") can be used as a supplement to the plethysmograph to detect arousal patterns in the general physiology as well as to detect "lies" and denial mechanisms.

Psychophysiological techniques provide useful information in the assessment process but may be even more useful in the treatment process. When used as an intrasubject measurement, the data can be used as a monitor particularly for behavioral treatment modalities. There may be considerably more validity to this approach. These data may also be critical in further research on normal and pathological response patterns.

Although these techniques are promising, there are important cautions and drawbacks to be recognized. Perhaps the most obvious is that a trained technician must administer the procedures. Besides the added complexity to the process, there is also the additional expense on top of a significant capital expense for the equipment (several thousand dollars depending on computerization options). There are also significant validity questions. Do we know enough about normal arousal? What patterns do "normal" subjects show? Does arousal predict behavior? If so, at what levels? What specific stimuli predict specific behavior?

Cautions Regarding Assessment

Assessment of accused or admitted offenders presents several unique problems. Primary among these is the dichotomy between subjects who talk "too much" and those who talk "too little." The latter is, perhaps, obvious. The subject may be facing a long prison sentence; loss of family, job, or financial security; and societal condemnation. Denial and minimization are frustrating but understandable and particularly painful when a child has to testify against a father. As prison sentences increase, the tendency, of course, will be toward more denial and less acceptance of responsibility. This affects all components of the system—from family to treatment to the criminal justice system to child protection agencies.

The other half of the dichotomy, talking "too much," is not anticipated by many counselors. There are many offenders, particularly within families, who eagerly confess to the pedosexual contact immediately on confrontation, and another group that will confess within a month of the report. Each of these groups may abrogate its own rights because of feelings of guilt and shame. In some cases, this is guilt that has been building or fermenting for years. Although this guilt release seems appropriate and could be therapeutic, it is also essentially irreversible and can result in later bitterness, resentment, and minimization.

Another caution is that despite the presence or absence of a "confession," there may be significant discrepancies in the reports, both being from one person to another and also from one time to another. These discrepancies may be normal and tolerated if they do not affect the overall responsibility issues. For example, specific dates, times, places, and frequency may be discrepant and acceptable if the nature of the behavior, extent, and duration are clear.

A typical confounding variable in the responsibility area is the claim of an alcohol- or other drug-induced blackout. Accused offenders will frequently claim vague or no memory of a pedosexual contact due to a "blackout." Some offenders will try to sidestep the responsibility issue by agreeing that they "might have" or "could have" done "something" or that "if *she* said I did it, then I must have." Others will totally deny memory and even use alcohol as a defense, claiming that they *could not* have offended because of lack of consciousness, absence from the home, or erectile incapability. Although the possibility of substance-induced amnesia should be acknowledged, many, if not most, of these cases do result in partial or total appropriate recall during the treatment process. While waiting for this recall, the offender's responsibility for the substance use/abuse should be a clear focus. If the denial process continues, the offender may not be a candidate for treatment.

The final assessment caution lies in the potential for manipulation by the subject. This caution is also applicable to treatment. The subject may well act charming, pathetic, or passive-aggressive in an attempt to ally with the examiner and convince him or her of the need for leniency. The manipulative behavior may also serve as a self-assuaging process, actually helping to convince the offender that the behavior was not harmful or serious.

Diagnosis, Categorization, and Treatment Planning

Assessment of the offender goes beyond the typical issues of diagnosis and prognosis. Risk assessment and treatment planning are both essential components and add to the complexity and difficulty of the task. Treatment planning should be considered even if incarceration is anticipated. Integration of diagnosis and pedosexual taxonomy category should be helpful, essentially adding three axes to the diagnostic system.

Most pedosexual behavior is not specifically classified in the DSM-IIIR. The exception, as noted earlier, is pedophilia, classified as 302.20 on Axis I as one of the paraphilias. The criteria for the diagnosis of pedophilia are quite specific although less so than in the DSM-III. There are three components:

A. Over a period of at least six months, recurrent intense sexual urges and sexually arousing fantasies involving sexual activity with a prepubescent child or children (generally age 13 or younger).
B. The person has acted on these urges or is markedly distressed by them.
C. The person is at least 16 years old and at least five years older than the child or children in A. (APA, 1987, p. 285)

The changes from DSM-III are:

- the duration criterion of 6 months

- "urges *and* fantasies" rather than "act *or* fantasy"
- "distress" can be substituted for action
- 16 years old as the minimum age
- focus on arousal instead of preference

These changes seem to have counteracting tendencies to be more inclusive (arousal, distress, possibility of nonexclusive behavior) and exclusive (duration, age, intensity).

Any of the other Axis I diagnoses of the offender are possibilities, but the most likely would be in the affective disorders, sexual disorders, or substance abuse. The diagnosis of an affective disorder is difficult because of reality influences and stresses and the frequent overlay of personality disorders. For many offenders, however, there is considerable depression, perhaps chronic, that could be diagnosed as dysthymia (300.40) or major depression (296.3x).

Although sexual disorders seem a reasonable corollary of pedosexual contact, they may not be more prevalent in the offender than in the nonoffending population. Possible disorders include other paraphilias, sexual dysfunctions (ejaculatory and erectile), and compulsive sexual disorder. The latter may fit for the addictive-type offender. Compulsive behaviors could include masturbation, use of sexually explicit media or prostitutes, voyeurism, exhibitionism, or a combination. These behaviors may not meet the criteria for paraphilias but still contribute to a compulsive sexual disorder.

Substance abuse may be a diagnosable condition. Careful assessment is essential in this area because of the impact on both risk assessment and treatment planning. Specialized treatment may be needed. Beer is most likely to be the substance abused because of the typical "macho" dynamics.

Axis II diagnoses are more typical for many offenders. Dependent, narcissistic, passive-aggressive, and borderline personality disorders, or mixtures of these, are likely. This kind of long-term pattern of behavior sets the stage for the triggering dynamics and disinhibition. The dependent personality in combination with dysthymic disorder sets up a particularly strong tendency toward poor self-esteem, lack of appropriate feelings of power and control, lack of affection and affective awareness, and use of alcohol or sexual behavior to fill other needs. Interestingly, antisocial personality disorder is not a typical diagnosis; most offenders have little or no history of overt antisocial behavior. They exhibit, instead, rather rigid, conservative/traditional tendencies.

Pedosexual Taxonomy

Pedosexual taxonomy can be a helpful framework because it focuses the dynamics of the pedosexual offender in a much narrower way than the DSM system can. Although, as noted, the five categories—regressed, pedophile, addicted/compulsive, rapist, symptomatic—are not completely discrete, I believe that they do separate out some factors that will assist in risk assessment.

Regressed. If the assessment does not indicate pedophilic patterns or other serious psychopathology, the offender probably fits the regressed category. There will probably be a reasonable psychosexual development with adult partners preceding the pedosexual contact. Dynamics include general stress, lack of control, poor self-esteem; history of physical or sexual abuse; marital/family dysfunction; and disinhibition factors, including alcohol use. There may well be a sense of "macho," a powerful veneer covering a sense of dependency and helplessness. Although this exists even before the pedosexual contact, it is worse after it, with the addition of significant guilt. That guilt, in turn, may trigger defense mechanisms, primarily projection and denial. Although the regressed offender presents a complex picture, prognosis for treatment is good if the offender accepts any responsibility for the behavior. Treatment will, however, be long-term and confrontive in order to deal completely with issues of responsibility, control, and power. If these issues are successfully addressed, the regressed offender will present a minimal risk of recidivism.

Pedophile. The criteria for DSM-IIIR diagnosis of pedophile also should be followed for the pedosexual taxonomy. Although the term "preferred" was eliminated in the shift from DSM-III to IIIR, it may still be a good operative word in exploring pedophile dynamics. Not only do pedophiles prefer children as sexual objects, they *generally* prefer to be with children and feel more comfortable with children than with adults. As one pedophile client succinctly summarized, "I love children. I *really* love children." Although criteria call for at lease a six-month duration, most pedophiles will acknowledge almost a lifelong preference (at least a general preference) for children. They frequently will present as kind, gentle, and generous individuals who may been seen as the best babysitter or caregiver in the neighborhood, giving gifts and taking children to the circus, zoo, and so forth. Although they may have had some adult sexual relationships, including marriage, they remain essentially asexual in regard to adults. Pedophiles may be more likely than regressed offenders to choose male children. Caution should be used with the term "homosexual pedophile" because the preference is very different than that of the adult homosexual. The pedophile may find great difficulty in focusing on responsibility and frequently sees nothing wrong with his behavior and sees no harm done to the children, frequently considering his gentle concern and affection toward children as superior to the childs' parents' hostility or apathy. Because of this difficulty with responsibility as well as the long-term preference, exclusivity, and urge intensity, the pedophile is generally seen as being at high risk for recidivism. Even when the pedophile is cooperative with treatment, mandated or voluntary, treatment efficacy generally has been poor.

The special case of the hebephile/ephebophile should be noted. For the purposes of the pedosexual taxonomy, these two categories are included in the pedophile area. These categories are not specifically included in the DSM-IIIR but are generally included in the paraphilias. Both are difficult to differentiate from normal arousal patterns because of our societal emphasis on the attractiveness of youth. The hebephile sees the female adolescent as having adult development but vulnerability. There may also be a sense of safety from rejection because the hebephile may have had actual or perceived poor sexual performance with adult partners. The ephebophile is even more likely to reflect the emphasis on youth in society; in this case, the gay culture's emphasis on youthful appearance. It should be emphasized, of course, that whereas many or most adults are attracted to the youthful appearance of the male or female adolescent, the hebephile/ephebophile not only takes action on that attraction but has a preferred or exclusive arousal pattern. In other words, whereas the societal youth emphasis is a factor in attraction to adolescents, it is not *the* reason for pedosexual arousal patterns. Unfortunately, the offender may well be use this as a rationalization and, like the pedophile, show little responsibility or acknowledgement of harm to the victim. Because of this, the hebephile/ephebophile also may present a significant risk.

Addictive/compulsive. The sex addict or compulsive is marked by the sense of a loss of control over sexual behavior. Any sexual behavior or combination of behaviors may be the compulsive focus. Masturbation and use of sexually-explicit media may be the most common behavior, with voyeurism, exhibitionism, and use of prostitution as other possibilities.

Other nonsexual addictions are likely, including alcoholism and eating disorders. Pedosexual contact may not be one of the most frequent behaviors among these offenders, but may become more of a focus as we learn more about the addictive/compulsive patterns. As mentioned, the sex history should bring out this information, although the emphasis should not be on either specific behavior or frequency, but rather on the sense of lack of control over the behaviors. With clear acknowledgement of responsibility (not only guilt or remorse), prognosis for treatment may well be good, particularly if specialized treatment is available. Even with this prognosis, however, there may be significant risk concerns. These risks may not be related primarily to the pedosexual contact but rather to other sexual and nonsexual risk behaviors, from voyeurism to drunk driving to cocaine sales to substance-related theft.

Rapist. The key behavior pattern of the rapist is violence. The typical risk dynamics of rape are magnified when we consider children as victims. Given our current lack of treatment efficacy with rapists in general, the pedosexual rapist is an extremely high-risk offender for both sexual and physical assault.

Symptomatic. Prognosis and risk assessment for symptomatic offender depend on the primary disorder. The frequency and type pedosexual contact may be strong factors, however, in risk assessment. As in other areas, the ability and willingness to take responsibility are major issues.

Treatment Planning

If the consensus of the evaluation, risk assessment, and the criminal justice system indicates treatment rather than long-term incarceration, the counselor may become a critical part of the treatment planning process. This process probably will be ongoing and integrated, with the probation department and Child Protective Services both likely to have input. Although the process will be dynamic over time, it will identify modalities, intervention approaches, and goals. Timelines, frequently used in treatment planning for other types of interventions, should be flexible and individualized. Regular treatment planning meetings, preferably formal and scheduled (with room for emergencies and crises), should be held to revise the treatment plan.

Treatment of the pedosexual offender is best when it is multimodal and when more than one therapist is involved. The presence of a therapy team discourages controlling and manipulative behaviors by the offender and the family and may improve both flexibility and accountability in treatment. Modalities include:

1. *Individual therapy.* The individual therapist may be designated as the primary therapist and should be the most stable, long-term influence. If possible, this person should be willing to commit to long-term (at least a two-year) direct and indirect involvement with the family. The individual therapist is also at the core of accountability.
2. *Family therapy.* Whenever possible, even if reunification is not a goal, marital and family therapy should be utilized. Family therapy can be supportive, confrontive, preventive, and curative. Cotherapy should be used when possible. Marital therapy should also include sex education and therapy.
3. *Group therapy.* Groups are essential in the treatment process for both support and confrontation (responsibility) issues. Groups can be segregated to offenders or, at a later point, include spouses. They should be homogeneous for pedosexual offenders and probably for regressed offenders as well.
4. *Self-help.* Many offenders and families gain socialization skills, practical and emotional support, and information from self-help organizations like Parents United. This group, founded in San Jose, California, as part of Giaretto's integrated treatment program (1982), now has chapters across the country, empowering families to help themselves, elect their own officers, and regain a sense of control over their lives.
5. *Educational groups.* Particularly in the later stages of treatment, educational groups can focus on issues like communication, parenting, and sexuality.

Specific intervention approaches include:

1. *Therapeutic-behavioral, cognitive, cognitive-behavioral, rational-emotive, and eclectic.* Behavioral (desensitization) approaches may include monitoring with the plethysmograph or other psychophysiological measures.
2. *Psychopharmacological.* This approach may include standard antidepressant and tranquilizer medication if appropriate, although few offenders seem to have received this. In fact, "self-medication," particularly

with alcohol, may be more likely than prescribed medication. One controversial treatment has been the use of an anti-androgen, medroxaprogesterone acetate (Depoprovera), sometimes called "chemical castration." Despite reports of success with some offenders, it is still generally considered a treatment of last resort.
3. *Probation.* Supervised probation is one of the interventions for many offenders. Although some clinicians may not see probation as an intervention in the typical sense, it clearly has major impact on the offender and his family, particularly as it applies to issues of power and control. Probation may be supervised at various levels of control, from monitoring by monthly report to surveillance and continued telephone accounting. Technological advances may include electronic "banding" and monitoring. The court will issue conditions of probation specifying restrictions on travel, visitation, and other behavior.
4. *Jail.* The offender may be ordered to spend some time in incarceration as a condition of, or precursor to, probation. Sentences may vary from 30 days to two years and may include special programs such as work furlough or weekday release to allow continued employment and family support. The imposition of "jail time" generally is intended to have a punitive, rather than therapeutic, effect, but it can be a significant intervention (positive or negative) regarding power and control issues.

Treatment goals ill vary, but certain goals seem consistent despite modalities and specific interventions. I have grouped these into six areas: responsibility, power, control, affective awareness, communication, and interpersonal relationships.

Responsibility. The offender will:

- clearly accept the responsibility for the pedosexual contact without reservation or rationalization
- clearly acknowledge the actual and potential harm to the victim, himself, and the family
- accept the ongoing responsibility for support and protection of the family regardless of reunification decisions
- demonstrate responsibility in employment, finances, and similar areas

- demonstrate responsibility in attendance and utilization of therapy opportunities
- accept and adhere to conditions of probation and other directives of the criminal justice and child protective systems
- differentiate between responsibility and guilt

Power. The offender will:

- acknowledge the appropriate power relationship inherent in the pedosexual contact
- identify and correct inappropriate power relationships in the family
- identify areas of individual powerlessness and plans for change
- assist in empowering the victim
- demonstrate ability to share power in the marital, familial, or work situation

Control. The offender will:

- demonstrate control over sexual arousal, behavior, and fantasy
- acknowledge disinhibitors and plans for controlling them
- describe the "set-up" for the pedosexual contact and plans for controlling these (relapse prevention)
- demonstrate general impulse control, including control over "temper" and substance abuse
- demonstrate control over day-to-day decision making for himself
- understand and resolve issues regarding need for control over others and relinquish this need

Affective awareness. The offender will:

- identify the full range of his feelings consistently and with understanding
- express the range of feelings and clarify same to the counselor and the family
- demonstrate ability to understand, clarify, and take appropriate action on others' feelings
- specifically, demonstrate ability to appropriately express anger

Communication. The offender will:

- demonstrate ability to use "I" messages and active listening
- demonstrate ability to express and receive thoughts, feelings, opinions, and beliefs
- develop effective extrafamilial communication (work, social, etc.)
- demonstrate improved parenting skills

Interpersonal relationships. The offender will:

- demonstrate improved relationship with spouse or significant other
- demonstrate awareness of intimacy needs within relationships
- show appropriate sexual relationship(s) with adult partner(s)
- demonstrate improved socialization skills and reduced isolation

Treatment

The assumptions in this discussion of treatment interventions are that most offenders will be *mandated* and available for *long-term* treatment. If either of those assumptions is not true, the treatment goals will have be modified, with an emphasis on crisis intervention, responsibility, and control. As in the treatment of victims, the stages of treatment for offenders are overlapping and flexible. Crises, for example, *will* occur throughout the process up to, and beyond, formal termination. The stages will be roughly parallel in either an individual or group modality.

Crisis Intervention

As noted earlier, all of the major family members (victim, offender, spouse) should be considered suicide risks. Even while denying allegations in the initial stages, the offender may attempt to resolve conflicting feelings by suicide. Clearly, any attempt could be devastating for the victim and family.

At the time of the report and arrest, more so than at later times, the offender is likely to perceive issues as "black and white." The counselor can use this black-and-white perspective with a clear treatment contract, including a suicide contract. Because many offenders have dependent features, the most effective suicide prevention may be in telling the offender, "Don't do it!"

For the most part, however, the counselor needs to emphasize and validate the gray area—that there will be few easy and clear answers. The initial crisis phase will be marked by extreme confusion and fear. Information received by the family will usually be ambiguous and elicit many questions—will the child be removed, the father arrested or prosecuted, siblings removed, the father incarcerated? The counselor will not be able to answer these questions and obviously should not make any promises about outcomes. In fact, the counselor should acknowledge and even emphasize that the family does *not* have control over these decisions but, rather, they have to focus their efforts on the small amount of control that they *do* have. This is a critical reframing.

As noted earlier, the offender is likely to enter this phase in a denial mode either by outright denial of the pedosexual contact or by minimization of the extent, frequency, duration, or effect of the contact. Even those who readily admit to the contact will have accounts that differ from the child's report, for many reasons. The offender can be supported in his need to protect himself while confronted about his need to accept responsibility for the good of his family and himself.

This concept of supportive confrontation is critical not only in this crisis phase but throughout treatment. The counselor must be able to support his or her client while still being able to confront the client on issues of responsibility, control, and accountability. The counselor consistently must walk the thin line of concern for the client and responsibility to the victim. One technique for accomplishing this is to ally with the offender in his concern for the victim. Most offenders are cooperative in this regard, making it somewhat easier to deal with responsibility issues.

As part the support, the offender can be assured that he is not the only one in this circumstance. Despite the heavy, negative societal condemnation and, more than likely, tremendous self-condemnation, the offender can be shown that his and his family's problems are not unique and that many families have recovered. Without diluting any responsibility for the offense, the counselor can show unconditional positive regard and reinforce the basic "OK-ness" of the offender. In most cases, the offender's lack of previous criminal record can be helpful, as can an emphasis on the previously mentioned alliance to protect the victim.

Once that support is given, responsibility becomes the biggest issue of the crisis phase. The offender *must* clearly accept responsibility for the offense. This is probably the most important treatment goal in the whole process. The responsibility must be unequivocal; that is, without excuses or rationalizations. The responsibility must go beyond a simple acknowledgement of the behavior. It must include the set-up, statements of threat, coercion, and confusion made to the victim, damage to himself and others, and consequences (jail, probation, separation of the offender's family). There can, and probably will be, specific differences in details between the "stories" of the offender and the victim. These differences can be explored during treatment *if* the basic responsibility is clearly accepted. The offender may need several sessions and considerable supportive confrontation in order to accomplish this.

The responsibility issue should be addressed in a positive manner, the emphasis being that responsibility allows the treatment process to begin. Responsibility, in a positive way, becomes the best route for the offender to take control of the treatment process and establish the first step in a more general positive control. The positive responsibility emphasis is in contrast to the disabling guilt that many, if not most, offenders feel. Although a certain amount of guilt is to be expected, it becomes self-destructive and counterproductive unless the counselor can turn it around into positive responsibility.

Apology Sessions

The apology sessions become the bridge from crisis intervention to ongoing treatment. The number of sessions and timing will be flexible. The goals will be responsibility clarification, apology, validation of the report, and commitment of treatment.

As noted earlier, the apology sessions will not take place until both victim and offender are prepared, with emphasis on the victim's safety and support. Preparation for the offender should focus on the responsibility issues and enough affective awareness to clearly respond to the offender for a variety of victim responses, from coldness to rage.

The offender will be expected to initiate the first apology session by acknowledging the complete responsibility for the offense and apologizing for the contact. The victim will then be encouraged to respond with feelings or questions. The offender *will* accept *any* feelings expressed by the victim. These feelings, of course, may be expressed over the course of several sessions. The other goals should be accomplished in the first session (although they may be repeated): The report should be validated as appropriate and the first step in "making things better," and the offender should make a firm commitment to treatment and to making whatever changes are necessary for the victimized family to recover and for the victim to be safe.

Continuing apology sessions should focus on including the rest of the offender's family, especially the spouse. Apologies should be directed to other family members, with clear acknowledgement of the harm inflicted. The details of the contact should be discussed in order to have an improved sense of protection and in order to disrupt the "family secret" pattern.

If the offender's family is not available for apology sessions, the process should still be completed using role-play (perhaps with another counselor) or letter writing. If only the children are not available, the apology sessions should be held with the spouse with, again, the details of the contact discussed, even if the spouse is not initially eager to hear them.

Pattern Analysis

Once responsibility issues have been clarified and communicated, the major treatment tasks involve pattern analysis. This includes an understanding of individual and systems dynamics, history, disinhibition, arousal patterns, and affective awareness.

As much as possible, the offender should bear the responsibility for work on pattern analysis. The counselor should facilitate the process and be accountable for progress toward the treatment goals, as well as for integration of the patterns.

The pattern analysis may be the biggest part of the jigsaw puzzle analogy mentioned earlier. The offender must painstakingly put together the puzzle, sometimes piece by piece, sometimes several pieces in a cluster. The counselor can understand how puzzles fit together but doesn't know how this particular one will look. And, the puzzle may never have all the pieces in place.

The first step in putting together the puzzle is to clearly identify the pieces. The offender must be able to discuss the details of the pedosexual contact and identify the direct antecedents to the contact. This is sometimes called the "set-up" or "seduction," although the latter is not an accurate description when viewed in the typical adult way. The details should include frequency and duration as well as progressive patterns (stroking to digital penetration to oral-genital contact). Victim and offender responses should be queried. Offender techniques for convincing the child not to tell should be elicited. Offender arousal patterns during the contact should be as specific as possible (how much of an erection, at what point, for how long?). Information regarding time and place will help to determine how protection mechanisms (e.g., rest of family) were circumvented. Finally, the offender should clearly understand how the report came about.

After the details of the contact have been determined, disinhibiting factors should be considered. These factors include any that clearly serve to disinhibit the offender from sexual contact with children. Disinhibiting factors may be relatively overt, like alcohol use/misuse; or more subtle, like elaborate rationalizations. The latter may include the child's "need for sex education," "need for affection," or "medical necessity." They also may include a child's initiating, enjoying, or demanding contact, spousal rejection, or the child's being asleep. One of the great ironies is that the offender could use the contact as punishment for sexual behavior such as normal childhood masturbation or peer exploration. Multiple disinhibition factors are likely to be present.

The disclosure of details and disinhibiting factors may take a considerable amount of time. Just like process of sorting out and turning over pieces of a puzzle, it may seem like a nonproductive and time-consuming effort, but it does unravel patterns and helps to "hook" the puzzle solver into the task.

One strategy for completing a puzzle is to identify the straightedged pieces and complete the outer perimeter. This accomplishes three purposes: It establishes the outer limits and dimensions, sets a structure for at lease some of the patterns, and provides positive reinforcement and encouragement by narrowing the number of possible combinations and by making connections. In the pattern analysis, this phase examines the individual's family and sexual history.

The offender will be encouraged to look at his family(ies) of origin with an emphasis on patterns of power, dependence, control, communication, discipline, and affection. The parental marital dyad will be discussed with an emphasis on models of affection, intimacy, and sexuality. Many offenders will describe a rather rigid, nonaffectionate family with either an absent or authoritarian father, physical abuse or, at least, a strong punishment orientation. In my informal clinical research, fewer than 10 percent of offenders have reported *any* physical affection from their fathers (hugs, strokes, shoulder pats, lap sitting). An autobiography may be a helpful technique in gathering this information.

The sex history should be structured so that the counselor can feel assured that it is as complete as possible. It seems obvious that the possibility of a history of sexual abuse should be thoroughly pursued. Many interviewers, however, end their pursuit by asking the question, "Were you ever molested or sexually abused?" Most offenders will answer this question negatively because they do not think of their early experiences as abusive. The more helpful prompt might be, "Tell me about early sexual experiences you had with an adult or much older child." This can be followed by a discussion of details and reactions, both past and current. The offender can be encouraged to reframe such experiences as abuse if the counselor considers it might be helpful. The sex history should also look at behavioral and fantasy arousal patterns, including masturbation and use of sexually explicit media.

The sex history and arousal patterns in most regressed offenders will tend to seem quite normal but limited. Homophobia is typical, as is a small number of close heterosexual relationships. Sexually explicit media may be a disinhibiting factor, but not to the extent that they are a factor for the pedophile or rapist and generally not with children as objects. Concerns to be explored fully include fantasy patterns involving children, adolescents, or particularly young or small women; also, fantasy patterns of control over partners, including instruction and experimentation. Force, if present, magnifies these concerns.

If arousal patterns, either during childhood or during the pedosexual contact, are of concern, the counselor might consider two options: psychophysiological assessment/treatment and fantasy control. In the former, the use of the plethysmograph can both assess and monitor treatment as a feedback measure. With or without the plethysmograph, arousal and fantasy patterns can be controlled through aversive conditioning (use of noxious stimuli such as smelling salts or use of visualizations), masturbatory satiation, or thought-stopping. Typically, these techniques would be utilized by specially trained therapists.

Once the background issues have defined the perimeter of the puzzle, the next strategy may be to group the puzzle pieces by color and shades of color to see if designs can be perceived. It should be noted, of course, that the puzzle process is not rigidly sequenced, so that some pattern/color grouping may occur while the perimeter is being assembled.

The colors are supplied by the awareness and clarification of individual and systems dynamics. Individual dynamics include personality and affective awareness and exploration of functional and dysfunctional behaviors. Typical dynamics include dependent and passive-aggressive personality patterns. These need to be continually challenged by the counselor, not in terms of right versus wrong or black versus white but in terms of productivity and effectiveness. Although all these dynamics may not need to be changed, offenders will have to become aware of their role in helping to set up or disinhibit the sexual behavior. Most offenders do change their behavior significantly, although they still may meet criteria for personality disorders. The *awareness* of these dynamics may be more important than major behavioral changes.

Along with recognizing behavioral patterns, the offender must be able to demonstrate affective awareness. It would not be unusual for an offender, when asked to describe a feeling, to respond, "I feel like it's all your fault." Integration of sensory and affective awareness may be a totally new concept as will the separation of thoughts and feelings. Many offenders report crying for the first time since childhood or for the first time *ever*. Permission to cry can be an effective lead-in to permission for feeling appropriately angry, sad, hurt, and so forth.

Dynamics may be important in any one of several systems that affect and are affected by the offender. The family system is obviously central, but employment, social, and extended family systems also may be important. The offender should become aware of roles, interactions, expectations, and other typical systems dynamics. One critical relationship issue should be stressed, however. The offender seems to have particular difficulty in handling intimacy, both within the marital or sexual relationship as well as in friendship and extended family systems. Concepts of vulnerability, trust, and openness may be difficult and require considerable counselor patience.

One last pattern to explore specifically is substance use/abuse. Not only should this pattern be looked at in terms of disinhibition but also in terms of personality, relationship, and lifestyle issues. Although most offenders may not have addictive patterns, at least not yet, substance use, particularly beer consumption, has a significant impact on isolative and insulative behaviors, passivity, rationalizations, and, of course, finances.

Throughout all this pattern analysis, as in the previous phases, there has to be a recurring emphasis on responsibility, power, and control. These three underlying factors may be the most important in initially having created the problem through their inappropriate use, in acting as change agents, and in ensuring the prevention of relapse.

Empowerment

Responsibility and control issues have been discussed with some emphasis. The third major factor, power, is frequently misunderstood because the abuse of power may, correctly, be one of the key factors in facilitating the pedosexual contact.

The inequity of power within the family is exemplified by the great irony of intrafamilial sexual abuse—the offender feels powerless for a combination of reasons at the same time as he perceives the child as powerful and tries to "fight fire with fire" by using sexual contact as a power tool—so, the powerless offender becomes powerful and then, after the report, again powerless. One of the major treatment task is to empower the offender in order to produce an equitable power balance within the family and improve related issues such as self-esteem, independence, and self-confidence.

Empowerment goes hand-in-hand with control issues. Independence and assertiveness can be encouraged through decision-making skills, option exploration, and negotiation skills. Within the family, particular attention can be paid to parenting and financial issues, both of which are closely identified with power. Outside the family, empowerment can take the form of outreach to others, either generally or specifically within the pedosexual self-help programs.

Career issues also can be the focus of empowerment. Many offenders have had a history of unemployment, underemployment, and serial employment resulting in both economic and psychological problems. Many also will lose their jobs as a result of arrest, conviction, or incarceration. Career exploration, decision making, and stability therefore become empowerment possibilities.

Termination

Even a seemingly clear-cut issue like termination is complex. There may be several different points that seem like terminations: family reunification, CPS case closure, "graduation" from self-help programs, release from mandated treatment, or release from probation. For our purposes, we will focus on termination from treatment, although the other points also deserve much positive attention.

Because most offender treatment is mandated, termination decisions involve more than the completion of treatment goals. The treatment team will have to agree, sometimes unanimously, on the demonstration of those treatment goals and, of course, be convinced the risk of repeated offense is minimal. The termination process may include an independent reevaluation, clinical or psychophysiological.

It should be emphasized that in assessing risk of repeated offense, the risk can never be considered nonexistent. Even in the best situations, the risk will be seen as "minimal." Essentially, the treatment team must determine not only an offender's consistent compliance with the treatment goals but also an ongoing commitment to change and self-monitoring. The offender should also be able to show an ongoing support system.

The offender's commitment should include a clear agreement to return to treatment after termination as necessary. The most successful cases in my experience have returned at least once after termination to deal with a new problem. In contrast, about half of the incidents of repeated offense occur after termination and all have been related to a resumption of substance abuse behaviors. If the offender remains on probation after termination, the probation department should conduct regular urinalysis and possible psychophysiological measures.

Other Pedosexual Forms

In describing treatment strategies, we have intentionally focused on the regressed offender because that is the type of offender most counselors and therapist encounter most frequently. Many of the same interventions are appropriate for other pedosexual offenders, but some specific issues should be emphasized.

Pedophile. Responsibility and control issues are critical with the pedophile and need to be emphasized in every session. If at all possible, arousal patterns should be consistently monitored. If treatment is to be successful with the pedophile, those patterns will have to be shifted completely. The pedophile will also have to alter his pattern of nonsexual contact with children, in most cases an extremely difficult task. Research in the treatment of pedophiles will have to continue from correctional facilities, with all of the attendant difficulties that entails.

Rapist. The dynamics of the rape situation and its issues of violence generally call for specialized training, based on the experience of clinicians in the corrections field (Groth 1979). although the dynamics of rape are becoming better understood, most offenders have difficulty acknowledging responsibility. Child rapists may be even more difficult to treat, although research does not indicate that clearly.

Addictive/compulsive. Treatment of the addictive offender is still in the early stages, but it seems that a "12-step recovery program" may be helpful and effective. Inpatient programs, similar to other addition programs, also have been established. For the pedosexual offender, coordinated treatment between an addictions specialist and the primary counselor seems necessary. As with the regressed offender, group treatment is helpful, if not necessary.

Symptomatic. The key element in treating the symptomatic offender is coordination between treatment team members dealing with the primary disorder and those dealing with the sexual contact. Clearly, the relationship between the primary disorder and the symptomatic pedosexual contact should be thoroughly understood.

Female offender. If there is one area that needs extensive research most, it is the phenomenon of the female offender. Although our data, as previously noted, continue to point to an overwhelming percentage of male offenders (with both male and female victims), clinical experience with adult offenders/survivors leads to the conclusion that many unreported contacts involve female offenders. Offenses by female offenders may still not approach the frequency of those by male offenders but may be more frequent than currently reported.

The major statistical factor, of course, is that male victims do not report as often as female victims because they are less likely to perceive pedosexual contact as abusive, and female children report abuse by adult women even less frequently. Many offenders report sexual contact as children from babysitters or aunts, but relatively few situations directly involving a natural mother. These situations seem to entail a major problem with substance abuse, leading to the conclusion that the offender was in a symptomatic pattern or that unusually strong disinhibition was necessary.

As an interesting sidenote, based on limited numbers, it has been our observation that female offenders are less frequently charged, convicted, or incarcerated. It is certainly not clear whether this is a pattern of reverse bias in the criminal justice system or a quirk.

Treatment of the female offender can be similar to that of the male offender. Typical issues of nurturance, intimacy, and dependency should be explored fully as should possible victimization history. Disinhibiting factors require extra attention. The basic goals of responsibility, power, and control are essentially identical to those for the male offender, although the female offender perspective in our society should obviously be taken into consideration.

Warnings and Cautions During Treatment

As noted in the assessment phase, the offender has many good reasons for denial and minimization of the offense as he faces sentencing. This continues to be a risk during treatment although less so after sentencing. What *does* continue is a tendency to *generally* minimize problems and emphasize progress in counseling. Vague comments such as, "I'm feeling better" or "Our communication has improved" or "I won't do it again" should be challenged and confronted with a statement like, "Tell me *exactly* how." Most offenders and their families (including the victim) are "ready" to terminate counseling after a few months, but when looking back with hindsight at the actual termination time, they see how much additional progress they have made.

A related issue is that an offender with a dependent personality will eagerly cooperate and say exactly what the counselor wants to hear. The offender's question, in fact, is specific: "What do you want me to tell you?" This, of course, fits right into the black-and-white, rigid pattern of the offender's pathology.

The length of treatment itself frequently becomes a therapeutic issue. The counselor will be under significant pressure to reduce the length. This pressure may come from the victim, offender, or nonoffending spouse. There also may be financial pressures on either the private practice or agency counselor to limit treatment duration. The best metaphor I've used to deal with this issue is that whereas 90 percent is wonderful as a "grade," this situation requires 99 percent, and that takes time, even beyond what seems like compliance with the treatment goals.

Reprinted from Intervention Strategies for Sexual Abuse, *by Robert Rencken, pp. 83-109. Copyright 1989 by AACD. Reprinted with permission. No further reproduction authorized without written permission of American Association for Counseling and Development.*

Perpetrators of Domestic Violence: An Overview of Counseling the Court-mandated Client

Anne L. Ganley

In September 1984 the Attorney General's Task Force on Family Violence issued a final report. This report, with its recommendations for law enforcement, prosecutors, and judges, calls national attention to a fact that victims and some communities have known for years—battering is a crime. It is a crime against an individual and it is a crime against the community. It is neither a private affair nor a family dispute. It is a crime that is destroying the bodies and spirits of its victims. It is a crime that is committed not by faceless strangers but by those closest to the victims. These perpetrators of violence are now being held accountable by their communities, and in increasing numbers some are becoming court-mandated clients in specialized counseling programs for those who batter.

Counseling the court-mandated client who batters is both the same as and different from counseling the noncourt-mandated client who batters. To understand these similarities and differences, one must understand the rationale for this intervention by the criminal justice system, the meaning of the term *court-mandated*, and the current thinking about the components of effective counseling for these clients. With this context established, the specific clinical and program issues of court-mandated clients can be addressed.

Rationales for Court-mandated Counseling

Court-mandated treatment for batterers has developed over the past five years as one of the interventions designed to end domestic violence and protect victims from further abuse. There are four primary reasons that communities have begun to utilize the power of the judiciary, in combination with the resources of counseling systems, to mandate perpetrators of domestic violence into rehabilitative programs. These four different but not mutually exclusive rationales emerged from the understanding that domestic violence is a public rather than private problem. They reflect new learnings about battering being criminal behavior, about certain characteristics of the perpetrator, about the impact of the family context of the violence on the victim, and about the social causes and reinforcers of battering.

First, certain communities have been recognizing that domestic violence—or at least some of it—is a crime (Soler and Martin 1982; Pence 1985; Domestic Abuse Project 1985) and as such is under the jurisdiction of the criminal justice system. Just as with crimes unrelated to domestic violence, the court's role is to hold the offender accountable and to determine the appropriate sentence. In sentencing, the court may mandate counseling in certain circumstances in order to rehabilitate the offender and in doing so prevent further commission of the crimes. Counseling or mental health treatment such as alcohol/drug abuse treatment, inpatient psychiatric care, and outpatient care, has been mandated for such crimes as shoplifting, arson, driving to endanger, driving under the influence of alcohol, robbery, indecent exposure, and embezzlement. In recognizing the criminal behavior of those who batter adult intimates as being no different than those same crimes against strangers, the court has as options for sentencing the same rehabilitative possibilities it utilizes with other offenders. While battering is not a mental illness per se, the mental health and rehabilitative intervention systems offer possible avenues to assist some individuals in changing their violent behaviors as well as the attitudes and beliefs that support such behaviors.

Second, certain characteristics of those who batter suggest that court-mandated participation in a rehabilitative program may be necessary for change to occur. Several authors (Bern and Bern 1984; Brown and Chato 1984; Ganley 1981; Saunders 1984) discuss those who batter as having tendencies to minimize and deny their battering behavior and/or to attribute responsibility for their behavior to persons or events outside of themselves. Examples of such minimization or denial include "it only happened once" or "it was just a little argument" or "I just shoved her" when a careful history-taking reveals that the "shove" was down a flight of stairs and the "little argument" resulted in hospitalization of the victim or the "only once" is once per month in a three-year relationship. The attribution of responsibility to events or others outside of oneself, also called externalization, is expressed in "she bruises easily," "she knows how to push my buttons," "I am under a lot of pressure," "the police officer was just out to get me," and so forth. When individuals deny or minimize their behavior or attribute its responsibility to others, they are unlikely to change that behavior. Through both the criminal justice process and mandated counseling, the court cuts through some of the minimization, denial, and externalization by holding the individual responsible both for his battering behavior and for changing that behavior so that future violence will not occur.

Another aspect of the externalization is the offender's tendency to be motivated externally rather than internally. Even with noncourt-mandated clients, the motivation for seeking intervention is often external to themselves, as in "wanting to get her back" or "my minister told me I had a problem." In the initial stages of intervention the client may often be more externally than internally directed. Eventually to remain free of battering behavior, the individual needs to develop some internal motivation for controlling his behavior. Because this takes time, the client may benefit from having an external motivator for going through the change process. The community, through its courts' mandating clients to rehabilitation programs, can become that external motivator.

Typically the victim has been expected to perform that role alone. But it is unrealistic to expect a person who is in crisis due to the violence of another to provide the consistent, external motivating force that those who batter need to make major changes. It would be like asking the victim of a mugging to take sole responsibility for influencing the mugger to change the mugging behavior while that victim is both recovering from the impact of the assault and is fearing another assault. It is the responsibility of the court, not the victims, to hold offenders accountable for their crimes and to require that the offenders complete the conditions of their sentences.

Third, due to the family context of the violence, victims of battering usually want somewhat different responses from the criminal justice system than do victims of crimes committed by strangers. While both sets of victims may want to be protected from further victimization and to have justice, they may define how to reach those goals somewhat differently. Victims of domestic violence crimes primarily seek an end to the battering through the rehabilitation of the offender rather than through revenge, punishment, or restitution. The victims of these crimes, unlike victims of crimes committed by strangers, have had or expect to have an ongoing relationship with their batterers. Regardless of whether they plan to continue the intimate relationship with the offender, they know that it is highly likely that they will continue to be in some kind of relationship with him because of shared children, relatives, property, history, or community. Victims of crimes committed by strangers are rarely confronted by such a continuance of the relationship. Victims of battering most often want the battering to stop and for the criminal justice system to accomplish that through rehabilitative measures rather than through punishment. Victims of violence committed by strangers usually want protection, restitution, and punishment. They are usually not interested in the rehabilitation of the offender or in keeping the offender in the community. In fact, they may look upon such efforts as being "soft on criminals." The intimate context of the crime of battering influences what the victims seek from the criminal justice system. Some communities have responded to that difference by developing a criminal justice response that emphasizes rehabilitation rather than punishment.

Fourth, because domestic violence is embedded in our social customs and institutions (Dobash and Dobash 1979; Schecter 1982; Straus 1976), it has generally been viewed as normative and acceptable. Battering results not from the specific interactions of a dysfunctional relationship nor from the stressors in life, but from the offenders' previous learnings about the use of violence and power in relationships (Ganley 1981). These learnings take place as the individuals interact with their families of origin, with society as a whole, and with specific personal experiences in their lives (Dutton 1984; Ganley 1981). These learnings occur through observation and through actual experience (Bandura 1973; Wiggins 1983). Significant progress in preventing battering, and specifically the violence against women and children, can only be accomplished if customs and institutions also change their responses to domestic violence. Court mandating clients to counseling to end their abuse of partners is one way to reflect a new social custom of not tolerating violence against wives or female intimates. Such an approach also brings together two major social institutions, the criminal justice system and the counseling field, in an active effort to work against battering. In the past both have either ignored or misunderstood battering, and in doing so they have reinforced and perpetuated the problem. Court-mandated counseling for the perpetrator of the violence then becomes one step to changing social customs and institutions that have supported domestic violence.

Meaning of "Court-mandated"

Counseling court-mandated clients raises certain issues for both those providing the counseling and those monitoring the offender. However before those issues can be addressed, the meaning of "court-mandated" need to be clarified and an overview of the specialized counseling approaches for the perpetrator of battering needs to be outlined. There seem to be several different popular understandings of the phrase "court-mandated," and the work with such clients may vary depending on what is meant by the term.

One definition—and probably the one most commonly used by criminal justice system personnel—is to be ordered or directed postconviction by the criminal court to follow through on certain conditions outlined in the sentence or the probation agreement. There are stated consequences if these court orders are not followed. For such court-mandated clients, counseling is then ordered as a condition of probation or as part of the sentence (sometimes combined with jail time, fines, restitution, community service time, ceasing contact with the victim, and prohibitions against further violent behaviors). Court-mandated directives may be monitored through an officer of the court or through a probation department.

A second understanding of "court mandated" stems from involvement in procedures that fall under civil court rather than criminal court jurisdiction. In these cases the orders or directives come from the civil court rather than from the criminal justice system. Protection orders, restraining orders, divorce, or custody determination are examples of procedures under the jurisdiction of the civil courts that may result in either requests or requirements for those who batter to complete counseling programs successfully.

A third category of so-called court-mandated clients are those who are referred as part of a pretrial diversion process. In the diversion programs the individuals are given the opportunity to have all charges dismissed by completing all conditions of the program (no further offenses, successful completion of a counseling program, etc.). In these cases the court is not mandating the treatment since diversion is an alternative to going through the prosecutory process itself. In fact, if an individual does not successfully complete such a diversion program, then the prosecutorial process is to be reinstituted. Only at that point does the court become involved directly. There usually is some monitoring system associated with such programs. With diversion, there has been no admission or determination of responsibility for the battering.

A final understanding of "court-mandated" actually concerns a misunderstanding of the term. To some, "court-mandated" is misunderstood to be any recommendation or suggestion by a member of the law enforcement or legal system. Therefore, there are clients who say they are court mandated to treatment because the arresting officer told them "to get help for their problem," or because their lawyer in a criminal or civil case told them to go to a batterer's program "to be evaluated for not really being a batterer," or their lawyer told them to go to an anger-control class "to improve their chances in court." With such clients, the suggestion is just that—a suggestion rather than a mandate of a particular court. The misconception stems from the belief that any act by law enforcement or the legal system is synonymous with a court action. A large number of clients report being court mandated who are actually only referred by someone from law enforcement or the legal system. A crucial point in understanding this type of a "court mandate" is that there are no legal consequences to the client for not following through with the suggestion.

Specialized Counseling Approaches for Men Who Batter

Specialized programs for men who batter adult intimates began to appear in 1977-1978 in response to the need to end the violence while also ensuring the safety of the victims. A variety of programs utilizing a variety of staffing patterns, intervention techniques, recommended number of sessions, funding sources, and so forth began to appear. While a detailed review of these programs (Eddy and Meyers 1984) is beyond the scope of this chapter, it is useful to describe generally the similarities of the approaches (Bern and Bern 1984; Domestic Abuse Project 1985; Edleson, Miller, and Stone 1983; EMERGE, Inc. 1980; Frank and Houghton 1983; Gondolf 1985; Pence and Paymar 1985b; Sonkin and Durphy 1982). This will provide a descriptive context in which to consider the specific issues raised by working with court-mandated clients.

Specialized programs for men who batter have some common characteristics (Ganley 1981). The stated primary goal of such programs is to eliminate the physical, sexual, and psychological battering used by the clients to control their intimate relationships. From this primary goal programs have developed lists of objectives such as, but not limited to, increasing clients' responsibility for their battering behavior, developing behavioral alternatives to battering, decreasing isolation by developing personal support systems, decreasing dependency on and control of person(s) they are abusing, increasing the appropriate identification and constructive expression of all emotions, increasing appropriate communication and problem-solving skills, and increasing their understanding of the societal and family facilitators of wife battering.

Client accountability for behaviors, emotions, and attitudes is central to the philosophy of counseling with these clients. Throughout the process, clients are held responsible for what they have done, felt, or believed as well as for what they are doing in the present and will be doing in the future. Client accountability is built into the counseling process in several ways: reports on behavior outside the counseling session; communication within the sessions; programs encouraging others to hold the client accountable; and measuring progress on what is observable, not on intentions or promises. Different programs will emphasize different dynamics as a way of assisting the clients in understanding their behavior, but all the specialized programs hold the client responsible for the battering behavior and responsible for changing that behavior.

Appropriate use of confrontation is crucial to altering the client's characteristics of minimization, denial, and externalization. It is difficult to change one's own behavior when one is not acknowledging it or is attributing responsibility for it to others. Programs take care in confronting the minimization, denial, externalization, and other self-destructive characteristics common in those who batter. This confrontation is done in a matter-of-fact way to educate the clients, rather than as a covert means of punishing them.

Psychoeducational therapeutic approaches are utilized by specialized programs for male batterers. This is due in part to the theoretical view that battering behavior results from learning rather than from biochemical genetic traits. Consequently, psychoeducational approaches can be used to alter those past learnings and to teach new behaviors and attitudes that will prevent further battering. Such psychoeducational approaches lend themselves to a structured format and a somewhat directive role for the counselor. They can accommodate a client population that includes a wide variety of personalities and life experiences more easily than can therapeutic approaches that rely on more homogenous groupings of clients. This is important since those who batter do not seem to have one specific personality profile. While no empirical research has at this date been completed to address that issue, clinical data support the hypothesis that battering is not associated exclusively with a particular personality structure. Furthermore, this client population includes those from various races, socioeconomic classes, educational levels, ages, religious affiliations, and occupations. Psychoeducational approaches that focus on changes in behavior, emotions, and belief systems have proven effective with this heterogeneous client population. (For one outcome study, see Program Evaluation Resource Center 1982.)

Groups are utilized by specialized programs for men who batter as the major format for therapeutic intervention. The rationale for using this particular strategy ranges from the practical (it is a cost-effective response to such a large number of clients needing intervention) to the therapeutic (groups provide a laboratory for clients' changing behavior).

Program and Clinical Issues

What is currently accepted as effective counseling for men who batter is applicable to the court-mandated client. One of the basic operating principles of the criminal justice system is that certain individuals must be held accountable for their acts against individuals and against the community. This process of accountability involves assessment (did the acts occur and under what circumstances?), adjudication, and consequences. Most simply put, the primary goal of the criminal justice system is to stop criminal behavior and to protect lives in the community. This is compatible with the programs for counseling those who batter, where the goal is to stop all battering to ensure the lives of all who are involved.

While some programs only serve the court-mandated client (e.g., MEN, INC. of Juneau, Alaska's program for the incarcerated offender; Duluth's Domestic Abuse Intervention Project; Brown and Chato's project through the Forensic Assessment Services of the Calgary General Hospital, Alberta), many other specialized programs for men who batter accept both court-mandated and noncourt-mandated clients. Whether or not the program is designed solely for the court-mandated client, the staff and clients must address certain issues. Some are unique to working with the court-mandated client; e.g., collaborative roles of the counselor and the criminal justice system, defining those roles to the client, information needed from the criminal justice system, information to be given to that system, and responses to the racism and classism of the systems. Some that apply to all clients who batter—e.g., victim safety, coordinating with victim services, ongoing assessment of lethality, reoffenses while in the program, client motivation for change, and evaluation of the program's effectiveness—must be responded to in particular ways when the program also serves the court-mandated client. Often there are no set prescriptions for responding to these issues, since laws and resources vary so greatly from community to community. What is important in working with the court-mandated client is that these issues be understood and addressed in order to increase the effectiveness of counseling and to meet the program's responsibilities to the community as a whole. Each issue will be raised separately, although in practice they are intertwined.

Collaborative Roles

Defining the collaborative roles of the specialized counseling program for those who batter and the criminal justice system is a matter of keeping clear with whom one is working and for what purpose. The previous sections outline some of the thinking that is necessary in working with the batterer, regardless of whether one is the counselor, prosecutor, judge, or probation officer. This section will now address the collaborative roles of the courts and the mental health system in evaluations for determining whether an individual is responsible for a crime, for predicting dangerousness to a community, and for determining the appropriateness of particular sentences. One note: Evaluation for the determination of responsibility or sentencing should always be kept separate from the evaluation for the purpose of counseling. This section deals with the collaborative roles in working with court-mandated clients postsentencing.

In the case of the convicted offender, the task of all is to hold the client accountable for what he has done as well as for the process of changing that behavior. Problems arise when the counselor or criminal justice system loses sight of that task or expects one system to be solely responsible for changing the offender.

Understanding each other's roles promotes collaboration. It is the responsibility of the criminal justice system to determine who is to be held accountable, to determine how that will be accomplished (e.g., jail, restitution, fines, community service, probation, rehabilitation programs), and to monitor that offender until he is no longer under the jurisdiction of the court. It is the responsibility of the counselor to determine which court-mandated clients would benefit from the specific counseling programs available, to provide that counseling as long as the clients use it effectively to stop the battering, and to provide specific information to assist the criminal justice system in its monitoring function. The criminal justice system may determine that a particular client is appropriate for rehabilitative programs according to its assessment of the offender and the criteria established for sentencing. Such a criminal justice system determination does not guarantee that there are rehabilitative programs available in the community that can provide counseling for all such clients. The counselor must retain control over who is admitted to the treatment phase of the program, since only the counselor knows the program well enough to know what will be effective with which kind of client. Given the scarcity of rehabilitative programs and the abundance of clients, this creates some tension between such programs and the criminal justice system personnel.

Another source of tension between the two systems is the monitoring function of the criminal justice system and the interface of that role with the ongoing assessment role of the counselor. In terms of monitoring, the criminal justice system has legal access to more information pertinent to the monitoring function than a counselor does. For instance, the criminal justice system has access to police reports and to other community members who may have knowledge of the client, whereas the counselor's information about the client is based almost solely on the interactions of the client with the program. Sometimes the counselor will have information from the victim, but that varies from program to program. Counselors are legally prevented from gathering the kind of information that is necessary to carry out the monitoring function of the criminal justice system. Thus the court must remain responsible for that function and not expect the counseling program to become the monitor. Certain communities have delegated the monitoring of abusers to a specific agency that is part of neither the counseling program nor probation department (Pence and Paymar 1985a). However, counselors do have some information that is pertinent to that overall monitoring function, and procedures must be developed for sharing that information. This sharing of pertinent information has to be recognized as ultimately being in the best interest of the client: his being held accountable for his progress is to his benefit. If it is not viewed by both systems in this light, then information may be withheld under the guise of client confidentiality. Suggestions of which information should be shared between the two systems will be given later in the chapter.

If an adversarial relationship develops between the specialized batterers' programs and the criminal justice system, it usually results from some confusion over who has what role with the client. Frequent communication between the two systems in a community clarifies the collaborative nature of their differing roles.

Specific Roles

It is important to define these collaborative roles of the counselor and the criminal justice system directly to the court-mandated client. In accepting court-mandated clients, specialized programs for men who batter are agreeing with the court that the client engaged in the battering behavior and that the client can change that behavior through participation in that program. If either is not the case, then it is best for the program to refuse to accept the client. The client needs to know how the two systems work together, what information will be shared and what will not be shared, and which system is responsible for which decisions. The counseling program is responsible for decisions pertaining to admission to, participation in, and termination from the counseling process, while the court is responsible for those decisions involving legal proceedings. These decisions may overlap at times, but they are not always the same. For example, the program may decide to terminate a client because he is not motivated to participate in the program, as evidenced by uneven attendance or tardiness. This information is given to both the client and the court/probation department. It remains the responsibility of the court or probation department to determine the next course of action. The court may refer the client to another rehabilitative program, or change the terms of probation, or refer the client back to the court for reconsideration of the sentence. The counselor cannot and should not be making that decision for the court. These differences in roles, as well as the overlapping responsibilities, need to be explained to the client.

Legal Records

To work effectively with the court-mandated client, the counselor needs certain information from the criminal justice system. The counselor should have on record the name, contact address, and telephone number of the person/office monitoring the client for the court. In addition, the counselor should ask that officer of the court for information on the charges filed against the client, the charges the client was convicted for, the sentence, and all conditions of probation (no contact orders, restrictions on alcohol or drug use, fines, restitution, etc.) including the length of time the client is to be under the jurisdiction of the court. If possible, information from the police report, court records, and presentence evaluation should also be made available to the counselor. It is also important for the counselor to know how the monitor will be carrying out that function (regular meetings with the client, information gathering contacts with victims or employers, etc.). Each community's system is somewhat different; when counselors work with clients mandated from different courts, it is important not to assume that there is consistency among the various courts.

Due to the client's minimization, denial, or genuine confusion about the criminal justice system, the client is not the best source of these facts. After gathering such information, it is often useful to review it with the client. If the client has questions about matters regarding the courts, he should be referred back to that monitor. The purpose of the review is to establish an openness for dealing with all information relevant to the battering and the court mandate. Some programs have developed a check list wherein such information from the criminal justice departments is systematically recorded for easy access throughout the process. Once the client has started the process, the probation officer or court monitor should inform the counselor of reoffenses or any significant changes in the client's legal status.

Counseling Records

At the outset of working with the court-mandated client, the counselor should establish with the monitor what and how information will be provided. For the most part, it is not appropriate for all the details disclosed by the client or gathered in the counseling process to be given to the court. Such details are often unnecessary to the monitoring function, although they are relevant to the counseling process. However, the criminal justice system does need certain kinds of information from the programs in order to make the evaluations necessary for the monitoring. The criminal justice system should be given a *brief* description of the intervention process: type of assessment, format of counseling, length of treatment recommended. In addition to this generic information about the program, the monitor will typically want to know attendance, reoffenses, and evaluation of progress.

There may have to be clarification between the court monitor and the counselor as to which reoffenses should be reported. A counseling definition of battering includes both behaviors that are illegal and some that would not be considered illegal. It is important that all reoffenses be reported to the monitor, even though when taken individually they may not be grounds for reinvolving the court. The reality is that battering is a pattern of behavior and the pattern can only be documented if there is a central place where the information is recorded. With court-mandated clients, that central place must be with the court monitor. Sometimes the counselor will hear of one seemingly minor event from the client, but information about it supports reports given to the probation officer by others not involved in the counseling. To work successfully with those who batter, one teaches accountability by not intervening between the offenders and the consequences of their behaviors. This means being willing to share information with those responsible for the monitoring. Just as in gathering the information, an efficient system for information exchange, complete with client-signed release-of-information forms, needs to be put in place. Since systems are useful only if used, the simple ones consisting of check lists or form letters or telephone calls are typically more productive. Regardless of the type, contacts between the criminal justice system and the specialized programs for men who batter should be documented in the client's records.

Racial and Class Issues

Working with court-mandated clients may bring the counselor into direct contact with the racism and classism of the criminal justice system. Like all other major social institutions in this country (including counseling systems), the criminal justice system too often reflects the racism and classism of this society. Its policies and procedures may discriminate against people solely on the basis of their class or race. In some communities, crimes will be differentially responded to by law enforcement, lawyers, judges, and corrections depending on the race and/or class of the individual. Court-mandated clients will bring their experiences of such discrimination into the counseling process. These experiences will affect how they view the rehabilitation program, which in their eyes may be merely an extension of the criminal justice system. In order to avoid perpetuating racism or classism, the rehabilitation program must ensure that its own policies and practices are not discriminatory. It must also be willing to acknowledge such racism and classism in the criminal justice system and work toward changing it by participating actively in community coalitions dealing with such problems.

In specific work with court-mandated clients, the program staff should be knowledgeable about the impact of cultural and class backgrounds on the experience of domestic violence, on the role of the criminal justice system, and ultimately on the counseling process. For some, their cultural background predisposes them to following the law of the land. For others, it increases initial resistance. The experience of racism or classism can be acknowledged without allowing it to become justification for their battering their families. Understanding the impact of racism or classism, as well as knowing the cultural backgrounds of clients, makes change more possible. The focus of the counseling should remain on helping the perpetrators stop their violent behavior against intimates.

Victim Safety

The most important issue facing programs for men who batter, whether court mandated or not, is the issue of safety for the victims. Stated simply, the issue is one of how to implement effective intervention for those who batter without further victimizing or endangering the victims of the violence. Understanding domestic violence for what it is—a pattern of behavior, not isolated or individual events, that occurs in an intimate and usually ongoing relationship—means that ensuring the future safety of the victims is a complicated task. A priority of abusers' programs must be to support the development and maintenance of shelters and safe homes for victims of battering. Without such sanctuaries, it is impossible to perform the information gathering and confrontation necessary to work through the offenders' minimization and denial. The first-stage interventions may themselves be stressful. Initially such intervention may increase the clients' feelings of helplessness. For those who batter, such anxiety is too easily displaced by increasing their control over victims through further physical and psychological abuse. Yet to change, the offenders must confront those anxieties. During that stage, victims and their children must have safe options in the community. Shelters are often the only means for that safety.

In addition to supporting services for victims, programs intervening with offenders need to monitor their own policies and procedures for their impact on the victims. The reality is that when we are counseling the violent offender, our client is not only that individual offender but also the family members and the community who have been his victims in the past and may be his victims again. Information from the victims is needed for accurate assessment and for appropriate monitoring. Respecting the confidentiality of the victim when getting her input is more than just a matter of respecting her individuality. It is often a necessity for protecting her life. Sharing information gained from the victim with the offender must only be done with her full consent and assessment of the possible consequences to her. A victim should be given accurate information about the intervention process in order for her to have realistic expectations about the offender's willingness to change or potential to reoffend. She should be encouraged but not coerced to participate in programs designed to increase her safety and her ability to take care of herself and her children.

Coordinating with Victim Services

In order to ensure victim safety, programs for men who batter must be coordinated with services for victims. Victim services include but are not limited to shelters, legal advocacy, medical services, counseling, community-based support groups, and advocacy and support projects for the children. In some communities (Pence and Paymar 1985a; Gamache, Edleson, and Schok 1984) the coordination of these services with those working with offenders is accomplished through systematic programs with paid staff to carry out the coordinating and monitoring tasks. In other communities this is accomplished through coalition meetings and informal communications among those working to end spouse abuse. Ending spouse abuse requires the resources of social activists, medical and legal systems, counseling projects, shelters, law enforcement, and religious and educational groups. This kind of collaborative work requires intentional effort and a willingness to develop trust based not on traditional credentials or signs of status but on skills and knowledge about ending battering. Just because a program is working with court-mandated clients and by its structure is connected with the legal system, it is not necessarily connected with victim services. Those connections must be actively sought.

Lethality Assessment

Given the life-threatening nature of some battering behavior, there has to be ongoing assessment of the lethality of the abuse. The issue of assessing lethality remains even after someone has been evaluated and admitted to a rehabilitation program. To assess the risk of injury or death occurring at a particular point, the counselor must know the individual's past history—severity and frequency of the violence; the presence of any interactive effects of alcohol, drug, or psychiatric impairment (psychosis or organic brain syndrome) with the battering; suicide attempt or threats by any family member; and the sexual or physical abuse of the children. The counselor must also evaluate the current status of the offender—his access to the victim, the suicide potential of any family member, current presence of stressors that the offender would typically have handled by battering his spouse, and the quality of his participation in the counseling program. The risk of injury or death may be low, moderate, or high at any given point in the rehabilitative process. When it is moderate or high, crisis intervention strategies should be used to prevent further violence.

Client Accountability

Since holding the client accountable is central to working with a man who batters, it is crucial for rehabilitation programs to develop consistent responses to the problem of the man who reoffends while in the counseling program. Given that battering is a pattern of behavior covering a wide range of physical, sexual, and psychological assaults, it is predictable that battering will reoccur during the intervention process. The legal process and the initial stages of counseling may not be sufficient to end the batter behavior of all court-mandated clients. In fact, some counselors report that there is often an increase in psychological battering when the physical, sexual, or property battering stops.

When any battering occurs, the counselor must respond to it in order to avoid colluding with it or inadvertently reinforcing it. With court-mandated clients, this information about reoffenses needs to be given to the individual doing the monitoring. Some of the reoffenses include criminal behavior such as physical assault, sexual assault, kidnapping, menacing, harassment, or crimes of property. Such battering must be dealt with by both the counseling program and the legal system. The response by the counselor or the officer of the court will vary according to the particulars of the reoffense. Responses may include confrontation and consequences: specified time out of the counseling program, changes in sentence, revoking of probation, charging and processing for new crimes, and so forth. For court-mandated clients, responses to the reoffense should be coordinated and not left the sole responsibility of one system or the other.

Client Motivation

Because of the minimization, denial, and externalization of those who batter, there is always the issue of increasing the client's motivation for change. Initially, clients may not identify what they are doing as being a problem, or if they see it as a problem they may not assume the responsibility for changing it. There is often an assumption that so-called voluntary clients have already worked through this minimization and denial and therefore are more successful in treatment than the court-ordered client. The alcohol and drug abuse treatment field has already demonstrated that success in treatment cannot be predicted by whether the client is court ordered or not. Some noncourt-ordered clients are very successful in making changes and some are not. The same is true for the court-ordered client.

With court-mandated clients, the issue of motivation for change is sometimes clouded by the particulars of how the client came to be identified as having a problem. The externalization typically found with those who batter may take the form of blaming the police, the prosecutor, the judge, or even the probation department for the problem. There may also be claims that the victim made the whole thing up. In states where there is domestic violence legislation, the blame may be put on the laws themselves. Having been through the criminal justice process, many of the clients approach the counselor with claims that they do not really have a problem. One way of responding to this is to clarify for the client that while he is court ordered into treatment, the program is not court ordered to treat him. Consequently, the client's role at this juncture in the process is to convince the counselor that he does indeed batter. Otherwise he will be not be accepted into the program and will have to accept other consequences for his crime. Note that the program is not designed to work with those who totally deny the problem nor to evaluate whether someone is battering. This clarification will often redirect the client's efforts away from minimization and denial. Another way to increase motivation is to listen to the client's description of the events and to assist him in identifying how his battering behavior is costly to him: loss of intimacy, impact on his relationship with children, friends' fear of his "temper," court costs, loss of work time, damage to property, loss of self-esteem, and so forth. Each offender is affected differently, and motivation to change must be initially nurtured by pointing out how it is in his self-interest that he stop his violent behavior. Pointing out these negative consequences is most effectively done in a group where the client can hear the comments of the others and start to develop new group norms that support being nonabusive.

There are advantages to working with the court-mandated client. The staff person begins the intake interview knowing that the client is a batterer and has had legal difficulty due to the violence. Such a client, when redirected into convincing the counselor that he should be accepted into the program, may in the process work through some of his denial. Many court-mandated clients will attend the first sessions regularly, thus giving the counselor some opportunity to deal with other aspects of the minimization or externalization. Noncourt-ordered clients may come only when there is an emotional crisis and quickly terminate when there is a superficial resolution to it. Also, with the court-ordered client there have already been some community sanctions placed against his violence; this is an important message in a society that still gives out very mixed signals about violence in the family.

Success in increasing the internal motivation to change in the court-mandated client often rests with the skill and experience of the counselor, If the counselor believes that court-ordered clients are more resistant per se, then clients will conform to that expectation. There are pros and cons to working with both sets of clients. Programs for counseling those who batter need to keep in mind that increasing and maintaining motivation change is an issue for all clients.

Program Effectiveness

Next to victim safety, the most important issue to be addressed by all programs for those who batter is that of evaluating the effectiveness of the intervention. Too often counseling is seen as a panacea. The reality is that it does not work for some clients, and at this point it is not clear with whom it might be successful. In this field, the successes of an intervention must be evaluated in terms of the impact that intervention has on the battering behavior. Does the battering end, decrease, remain the same, or increase following the intervention? Since battering is a behavior problem that can become habituated, an additional question concerns how long the change lasts. To answer such questions, information first needs to be systematically gathered at intake in order to have baseline data about the physical, sexual, psychological, and property battering committed by the offender against family members and those in the community. Such information must be gathered from several sources, including the victims. These measures should be administered again during counseling, at termination, and in follow-up intervals of six months, one year, three years, and five years.

With limited funds and the large demand for the development and maintenance of intervention programs for the perpetrator, the systematic information gathering needed for outcome studies has often been overlooked. As curricula have been designed ind intervention programs stabilized, more attention is being directed toward those basic outcome studies. The gathering of reliable and valid data is costly in staff time, especially in the initial stages of developing appropriate methodology. For programs that have not conducted outcome studies, it is better to start with simple designs that can be expanded upon rather than to attempt an elaborate design with insufficient resources for carrying it out. Regardless of the size of the project, a crucial step is to put in place a system for gathering the intake data integral to outcome studies. This establishes the mechanism for conducting follow-up studies, when additional resources become available, on representative samples of clients participating in the program. With programs open to court-mandated clients, there is particular interest in the evaluation of rehabilitative counseling versus other consequences imposed by the legal system. As in all outcome studies, the information gathered can be used to improve the effectiveness of the intervention by providing the data needed for program monitoring.

Beyond Counseling

Counseling the court-mandated client who batters represents a major shift in our understanding of the community role in addressing the problem of battering. Violence against intimates is no longer to be tolerated, and all the community's resources should be utilized to develop a wide variety of interventions for this problem. Intervention with the offender must include specialized counseling programs, but ultimately must not be limited to them. Counseling is always rehabilitation, and for prevention to occur attention must be given to how we socialize future generations to live in intimate relationships.

References

Attorney General's Task Force on Family Violence, Final Report, September 1984. Washington, D. C.: U.S. Attorney General.

Bandura, A. 1973. *Aggression: A social learning analysis.* Englewood Cliffs, N. J.: Prentice-Hall.

Bern, E., and L. Bern. 1984. A group program for men who commit violence to their wives. *Social Work With Groups* 7(1): 63-76.

Brown, R. J., and F. L. Chato. 1984. *Characteristics of wife batterers and practice principles for effective treatment.* Calgary, Alberta: Forensic Services, Calgary General Hospital.

Dobash, R. E. and R. Dobash. 1979. *Violence against wives.* New York: Free Press.

Domestic Abuse Project. 1985. Intervening in women abuse: A total systems approach. Minneapolis, Minn.: Author.

Dutton, D. G. 1984. A nested ecological theory of male violence towards intimates. In P. Caplan (ed.), *Feminist Psychology In Transition.* Montreal: Eden Press.

Eddy, M.J., and T. Myers. 1984. *Helping men who batter: A profile of programs in the U.S.* Texas State Department of Human Resources.

Edleson, J., D. Miller, and G. Stone. 1983. Counseling men who batter: Group leader's handbook. Albany, NY: Men's Coalition Against Battering.

EMERGE, Inc. 1980. *Organizing and implementing services for men who batter.* Boston: Author.

Frank, P., and B. Houghton. 1983. *Confronting the batterer: A guidebook to creating the spouse abuse educational workshop.* New City, NY: Volunteer Counseling Service.

Gamache, D. J., J. L. Edleston, and M. D. Schok. 1984. *Coordinated police, judicial and social service response to woman battering: A multiple-baseline evaluation among three communities.* Minneapolis: Domestic Abuse Project.

Ganley, A. 1981. *Court-mandated counseling for men who batter: A three day workshop for mental health professionals.* Washington, D. C: Center for Women Policy Studies.

Gondolf, E. 1985. *Men who batter: An integrated approach for stopping wife abuse.* Holmes Beach, Fla.: Learning Publications.

Pence, E., and M. Paymar. 1985a. *Domestic abuse intervention project: Curriculum for men who batter.* Duluth, Minn.: Domestic Abuse Intervention Project.

Pence, E., and M. Paymar. 1985b. *Criminal justice response to domestic assault cases: A guide for policy development.* Duluth: Domestic Abuse Intervention Project.

Program Evaluation Resource Center. 1982. *Exploratory evaluation of the domestic abuse project.* Minneapolis: Author.

Saunders, D. 1984. Helping husbands who batter. *Social Casework: The Journal of Contemporary Social Work*:347-353.

Schecter, S. 1982. *Women and male violence.* Boston: South End Press.

Soler, E., and S. Martin. 1982. *Domestic violence is a crime.* San Francisco: Family Violence Project.

Sonkin, D., and M. Durphy. 1982. *Learning to live without violence: A handbook for men.* San Francisco: Volcano Press.

Straus, M. A. 1976. Sexual inequality, cultural norms, and wife beating. *Victimology* 1:54-76.

Wiggins, J. A. 1983. Family violence as a case of interpersonal aggression: A situational analysis. *Social Forces* 62(1): 102-123.

From Domestic Violence on Trial. *Daniel Jay Sonkin (ed.). Copyright 1987 by Springer Publishing Company, Inc., New York 10012. Used by permission.*

Influencing Reluctant Elderly Clients to Participate in Mental Health Counseling

Floyd F. Robison, Marlowe H. Smaby, Gary L. Donovan

The current cohort of elderly adults has been described as reluctant to participate in mental health counseling services (Ganikos 1979; Ponzo 1978), despite recent estimates (Butler and Lewis 1982; Johnson and Riker 1982; Meyers and Loesch 1981) that many elderly persons experience significant mental health needs. The term *reluctant* is used here to describe elderly persons who do not seek or accept counseling services or, when they are in counseling, appear resistant or unmotivated to act on their concerns (Ponzo 1978; Waters 1984).

Several reasons may account for reluctance among elderly persons who are offered mental health counseling services. Many older persons are reluctant to define their problems in mental health terms because they perceive a stigma associated with such services (Herr and Weakland 1979; Lawton 1978) or because they believe that their participation in counseling may be an initial step toward institutionalization (Ganikos 1979). In addition, some elderly persons may be reluctant to participate in counseling because they believe they are "too old" or lack material and personal resources needed to effect change (Colangelo and Pulvino 1980; Kastenbaum 1968; Ponzo 1978; Peters 1971; Riker 1981). Finally, many elderly persons may resist disclosing personal information to a counselor (particularly a much younger counselor) if they believe that counselors do not have the breadth and similarity of experiences needed to understand their concerns (Blake and Bichekas 1981; Waters 1984).

We propose that mental health counselors can reduce elderly persons' reluctance to participate actively in counseling through the planned use of their professional power and influence. This article will describe several interventions to reduce reluctance by influencing elderly clients' perceptions of counselors' attractiveness, expertness, and trustworthiness.

These interventions are presented within the conceptual framework of the Power Strategies Model (Smaby, Peterson, Tennyson, and Tamminen 1988). The model describes influencing strategies that may be used in three types of professional relationships. After briefly reviewing the literature on power and influence in counseling relationships, this article will describe the Power Strategies Model and its implications for influencing reluctant elderly clients in mental health counseling contexts.

Power and Influence in Counseling

Several writers have offered definitions of the term *power*, and a consistent theme in these definitions is that power is the ability of one party to influence another. Nyburg (1981) defined power as the production of planned influence, whereas McClelland and Burnham (1979) asserted that power is a desire to be strong, impactful, and influential in relationships with others. More recently, Smaby et al. (1988) defined power as the capacity to influence persons and/or events in ways that alter the patterns of relationships between individuals. This definition places power and influence in an interactional perspective, in that one party's power to influence another is affected by the other party's power.

Atkinson and Wampole (1982) identified three elements of power and influence within counseling relationships. These elements are attractiveness, expertness, and trustworthiness. As defined by Atkinson and Wampole, attractiveness is a client's perception of a counselor as approachable and friendly. Expertness is defined as the client's perception of the counselor as having specialized training and skill, while trustworthiness is defined as the perceived openness, dependability, and sincerity of the counselor. Atkinson and Wampole suggested that a counselor's ability to influence a client is related to the degree that the client perceives the counselor as having these characteristics.

Given the association between power and these three relationship elements, Smaby et al. (1988) developed the Power Strategies Model to assist counselors in selecting strategies to influence others (e.g., clients) according to the levels of attractiveness, expertness, and trustworthiness present in their relationships.

The Power Strategies Model

The Power Strategies Model (Smaby et al. 1988) describes influencing strategies in four types of professional relationships labeled indirect, reciprocal, expert, and referent. These four relationships are distinguished according to the levels of perceived expertness, attractiveness, and trustworthiness between the parties. In three of these relationships (referent, expert, reciprocal), there are strong, moderate, or limited degrees of perceived attractiveness, expertness, and trust between parties. Smaby and his colleagues suggest that counselors can use direct influencing strategies in these relationships. The fourth type of relationship (indirect) involves the use of indirect influence, based on the absence of perceived expertness, attractiveness, or trustworthiness. Because Smaby et al. did not recommend the use of indirect influencing strategies in counseling relationships for ethical reasons, it will not be described further here. (For a complete description of indirect influencing strategies, see Smaby et al. 1988.)

According to Smaby and colleagues (1988), reciprocal relationships are based on mutual exchanges between a counselor and another person (e.g., a client), in which each party feels motivated to give in return for what has been received from the other. The two parties perceive each other as have little attractiveness, expertness, or trustworthiness. Actions taken in the relationship are not based on perceptions of mutuality, identification, reliability, or similarity. Rather, the relationship operates through each party's power to provide an immediate service, or meet an immediate need, of the other. Likewise, each party is motivated to respond to the other by a desire for the other to meet immediate needs.

Smaby et al. (1988) asserted that a counselor who has established an expert relationship with a client is perceived as having moderate levels of trustworthiness and attractiveness and moderate to high levels of expertness. In this situation, the client appreciates the counselor's training, experience, accomplishments, and skills, while the counselor likewise appreciates the client's experiences, resources, and capacity for change. Thus, the relationship is maintained primarily by mutual respect, rather than by mutual liking or high levels of interpersonal trust. Each party is motivated to respond to the other out of faith in the other's skills and knowledge and a desire to benefit from the skills and knowledge.

As defined by Smaby et al. (1988), a referent relationship is one in which the counselor and client experience strong mutual feelings of trust, expertness, and attractiveness. The parties respect each other on the basis of their perceptions of similar aspirations, achievements, characteristics, and experiences. Moreover, Smaby et al. suggest that referent relationships are characterized by high levels of identification, co-modeling, and mutual support. The parties feel free to confront each other directly and negotiate more widely discrepant approaches to problem situations without discomfort that they will lose the other's respect. In this type of relationship, each party is motivated to respond to the other by mutual respect, trust, and liking and by a desire to maintain the relationship.

In this model, the three power relationships are conceptualized as a developmental hierarchy, with reciprocal relationships at the lowest level and referent relationships at the highest level. As the relationship becomes more sophisticated, it would be expected that each party would become more motivated to respond in ways desired by the other.

The following paragraphs describe interventions derived from the Power Strategies Model that counselors can use to reduce reluctance in elderly clients by increasing elderly clients' perception of them as attractive, expert, and trustworthy. Some of the interventions described below have been suggested in the literature previously and are presented here to integrate them with the Power Strategies Model. Other interventions are suggested from our experiences as counselors with elderly clients and supervisors of mental health counselor trainees who worked with older persons.

Implications for Influencing Reluctant Elderly Clients

Influencing Strategies in Reciprocal Relationships

Generally, we have found that when an elderly client appears reluctant to participate in mental health counseling, the relationship is at the reciprocal level. The client may be resistant or unmotivated to talk with the counselor, and the counselor may, in turn, view the client as uncooperative, frustrating, and difficult. In reciprocal relationships, counselors may use several interventions to decrease elderly clients' reluctance to participate in counseling. These interventions are described below.

Self-disclosing to promote similarity. Several writers (Corey 1985; Corey and Corey 1987, pp. 345-374; Egan 1982; Ivey 1980) have suggested that judicious use of self-disclosure by counselors can promote initial rapport with clients. We have found that mental health counselors can use self-disclosure to promote a perception of themselves as similar to elderly clients that, in turn, enhances clients' perception of counselors' attractiveness. Further, we have observed that the most effective types of early counselor disclosures emphasize similarities of experiences and backgrounds (e.g., having children, living in a particular area of the country, educational and occupational experiences). Disclosures of a more personal nature are best reserved for more advanced stages of relationship development, as intimate disclosures may be perceived as threatening (Blake and Bichekas 1981).

Advocacy/advising on less threatening concerns. In our work with elderly persons, we have found that a client who initially is reluctant to discuss emotional or interpersonal concerns often is receptive to receiving help with more immediate, practical concerns. We suggest that dealing with the client's immediate needs reduces reluctance in the following ways:

- by demonstrating a sincere willingness to help the client
- by communicating that the client is attractive
- by exhibiting trustworthiness by being available to advise the client or by following through with an offer to advocate for the client to others
- by providing help in a nonthreatening way
- by acknowledging the client's ability (i.e., expertise) to act positively on concerns
- by demonstrating trust in the client
- by demonstrating expertise to the client in dealing with concerns

In turn, the client would be expected to perceive the counselor as increasingly attractive, trustworthy, and expert and to experience motivation to raise other problem areas for discussion.

Using reflective listening to build trust. Several writers (Blake and Bichekas 1981; O'Brien, Johnson, and Miller 1979; Waters and Weaver 1981) have suggested that reflective listening is an important intervention skill for building an initial rapport with an elderly client. From the perspective of the Power Strategies Model, we believe that reflective listening also communicates the counselor's willingness to "move at the client's pace" in pursuing problem areas rather than immediately attempting to diagnose and rectify a "psychological problem." In addition, we have found that counselors who take time to listen and talk to elderly persons about themselves and their experiences tend to be perceived as personally interested in the client, and, therefore, more attractive and trustworthy.

Minimizing direct confrontations. We have found that, in reciprocal relationships, counselors should avoid strong, direct confrontations of elderly clients' ideas or resistance to change. Although confrontation is a highly effective therapeutic tool in relationships characterized by mutually perceived trust and attractiveness, confrontation tends to be viewed as an attack and a sign of insensitivity by elderly persons who have not yet attributed those characteristics to their counselors (Herr and Weakland 1979; Waters and Weaver 1981).

Communicating at the client's level of understanding. Herr and Weakland (1979) suggested that many elderly clients feel threatened by clinicians' use of psychological jargon during counseling interactions. We have found that although the use of a professional manner when interacting with older clients increases their perception of counselors' expertness, counselors can concurrently enhance clients' perception of them as similar by adjusting their interaction style (i.e., choice of words and phrases) to that of clients. This process of adopting clients' communication styles has been described by systems-oriented family therapists as "accommodation" (Minuchin 1974).

Strategies to Develop Expert Relationships

In addition to the strategies above, we have found that several techniques described in the Power Strategies Model can be adapted by mental health counselors to develop relationships with reluctant elderly persons from the reciprocal level to the expert level. These techniques include (a) maintaining a professional appearance, (b) describing to the older clients situations in which other elderly persons have been helped with similar concerns (taking care not to disclose identifying information about other clients), (c) making references available to clients from other professionals who are acquainted with the counselor's expertise and in whom the client perceives expertness, attractiveness, and trust-worthiness, (d) demonstrating knowledge and skills through workshops and other educational programs in settings where current and prospective clients may observe the counselor's expertise, (e) addressing older clients by their titles (e.g., Mrs. Smith, Mr. Jones) unless permission is obtained to use the first name, (f) allowing clients to address the counselor by title rather than first name, even if the counselor should prefer being called by the first name, and (g) using tactful, polite communication.

Influencing Strategies in Expert Relationships

When a counselor has developed greater levels of perceived trustworthiness and attractiveness with an older client, and a moderate level of expertness has been established, the counselor's influence is derived from the client's willingness to accept the expertise (Smaby et al. 1988). Strategies to increase motivation within expert relationships are described below.

Making mildly discrepant statements regarding change. According to Smaby et al. (1988), a mildly discrepant statement is a form of mild confrontation through which the counselor suggests ideas that are slightly different from the client's ideas. Mildly discrepant suggesting is similar to the technique of reframing (Haley 1976). When proposing ideas that are only mildly discrepant from those of the client, the counselor acknowledges the client's ideas as valid while proposing new ideas that are not substantially different and thus are more likely to be accepted and acted upon (Herr and Weakland 1979; Smaby et al. 1988).

Explaining psychological processes. We have found that mental health counselors in expert relationships with elderly clients can reduce reluctance to consider alternative problem-solving approaches by discussing their conceptualizations of clients' concerns and explaining the reasons for their interventions. By explaining the conceptual bases for interventions, counselors can acknowledge clients' ability to understand their own concerns. In turn, clients are more likely to respect their counselors' understanding and insight and respond more positively to therapeutic suggestions. As described above, counselors' explanations of reasons underlying problems should be only mildly discrepant from the client's explanations and should be communicated in language that clients can understand readily.

Identifying clients' resources/skills for change. Elderly clients often are reluctant to attempt change in their lives because they are not aware of their personal resources to cause desired changes or because they underestimate the value of their resources (Lombana 1976). We propose that, in expert relationships, mental health counselors can influence elderly clients by suggesting ways that clients can draw upon material, human, and personal resources to act on their concerns. Likewise, counselors can help the client identify realistic limits on types of change that can be achieved and suggest ways the client can obtain needed resources. By identifying available and attainable resources and acknowledging that there may be limits to the amounts and kinds of change that clients can cause, counselors can communicate that they are sensitive to the realities of clients' situations and that their interventions take into account the types of resources clients have available.

Using peer models to instill hope. It is sometimes possible to work with a reluctant elderly client with the assistance of another person who is the same age as the client and has dealt successfully with similar types of concerns (Waters and Epstein 1980; Waters, Reiter, White, and Dates 1979). The counselor can use the "age confederate" as a model for more effective ways of construing the problem, identifying available resources for change, and identifying potentially effective problem-solving strategies. Moreover, we have found that although a counselor may not yet have established a sufficiently cohesive relationship with an elderly client to directly confront maladaptive or hopeless thinking, the peer is often in a position to confront, because of similarity to the client in age and experiences. Group counseling is another effective means of linking a client with peers. The opportunity for interpersonal learning from similar peers is an important reason that group counseling tends to be the treatment mode of choice with many elderly persons (Corey and Corey 1987, pp. 345-374).

Influencing Strategies in Referent Relationships

Smaby et al. (1988) asserted that parties in referent relationships perceive each other as highly attractive, expert, and trustworthy. They suggested that, in such an environment, the parties expect each other to communicate ideas honestly and directly. Accordingly, we believe that mental health counselors in referent relationships can maintain elderly clients' motivation to cause change by using the following interventions.

Challenging and participating. In referent relationships, we have found that counselors can maintain elderly clients' motivation by directly challenging them to act upon their concerns and offering ideas for change that are more widely discrepant from their ideas. By challenging clients to generate change strategies and act on them, counselors communicate confidence in the relationships and reaffirm sincere respect and caring for their clients.

Increasing counselor transparency. Earlier, we suggested that by disclosing selected information about personal characteristics, past experiences, and present life situations, mental health counselors can emphasize their similarities to elderly clients. In referent relationships, we have often found it useful and desirable to judiciously disclose more personally significant information about ourselves to elderly clients. Such information may include (a) our own feelings and thoughts about interpersonal situations in our lives, (b) personal concerns and ways we are attempting to resolve them, and (c) immediate feelings and thoughts about our relationships with clients. Blake and Bichekas (1981) have suggested that these types of counselor disclosures can benefit elderly clients in several ways: (a) by describing problem-solving behaviors that clients may adapt to their situations and use to generate further problem-solving alternatives, (b) by reaffirming trust in clients, (c) by helping clients realize that they are not unusual in having their concerns, and (d) by communicating genuineness to clients. However, counselors must ensure that their disclosures are intended to enhance clients' progress toward therapeutic goals rather than to achieve dramatic effect or to meet the counselor's emotional needs (Corey 1985; Egan 1982; Dies 1973; Ivey 1980).

Involving clients as helpers to others. We have observed that as elderly persons successfully progress toward their change goals, they often become interested in helping others. Being helpful to others enhances elderly persons' self-esteem and sense of personal power, as has been found in evaluations of peer counseling projects (Bratter and Tuvman 1980; McCaslin 1983; Waters et al. 1979) and, more recently, a "telephone visitor" program (Robison and Robison 1989). We therefore suggest that mental health counselors in referent relationships with elderly clients encourage their clients to enter into helping relationships with others, particularly relationships through which the client and counselor can collaborate as helpers (e.g., through co-counseling or with the counselor as consultant to the client-helper).

Summary and Conclusions

This article describes several interventions to reduce reluctance in elderly clients based on the use of planned professional influence. At the outset of counseling, elderly persons may perceive mental health counselors as low in credibility, expertness, and trustworthiness and yet respond positively to efforts to help them meet immediate needs that may be viewed as "nonpsychological" in nature. By using influencing interventions associated with reciprocal relationships, we suggest that counselors can increase clients' motivation to participate in counseling and enhance clients' perception of them as attractive, expert, and trustworthy. As the relationship progresses, counselors can further use their influence to develop expert and, eventually, referent relationships, with related increases in the quality of clients' participation. However, although we encourage the use of influence to obtain elderly clients' participation in counseling, we acknowledge that the effectiveness of influencing interventions may vary according to counselors' motivations for using them.

The use of interpersonal influence when counseling older persons may raise ethical issues concerning whether it is a selfish manipulation of clients (Kotter 1979). Such concerns may be particularly significant when counseling elderly persons who are vulnerable to the actions and influence of others. However, a number of writers (Corrigan, Dell, Lewis, and Schmidt 1980; Goodyear and Robyak 1981; Heppner and Dixon 1981; Johnson and Matross 1977; Strong 1978) have argued that interpersonal influence is an integral and desirable component of the counseling process. These writers have stressed that in order for counselors to use their influence ethically, they must be aware of their motives for influencing clients and sensitive to effects of their influence on clients' decisions. In this regard, the Power Strategies Model conceptualizes influence in counseling relationships as an interactive process, meaning that counselors who wish to be perceived as attractive, expert, and trustworthy must genuinely perceive these characteristics in their clients. Consequently, we assert that if counselors are to successfully use influence to obtain elderly clients' cooperation, they must be sincere when communicating interest in the welfare of their clients.

Our evaluations of these interventions have been limited to informal data gathering from our clients, members of their families, and social agency and health care workers who have provided referrals. During a two-year period since beginning the development of this approach, we have observed increases (ranging from 30 to 50 percent) in the proportion of clients age 65 years and older in our private practice and community agency caseloads. In addition, client reports of satisfaction with counseling services have been consistently favorable, and social agency and health care caseworkers have reported improvement in our older clients' levels of functioning upon termination of counseling. Because these data have been collected from a limited, nonrandom sample and are based largely on self-reported outcomes, our findings certainly are not sufficient to establish the effectiveness of these interventions. However, we believe such data are encouraging and provide a basis for conducting more extensive evaluation research. In addition, it is our intent that the influencing strategies presented here will serve as a foundation for mental health counselors to refine the various influencing interventions and integrate additional interventions within the model.

References

Atkinson, D., and B. Wampole. 1982. A comparison of the Counselor Rating Forms and the Counselor Effectiveness Rating Scale. *Counselor Education and Supervision* 22:25-36.

Blake, R. H., and G. Bichekas. 1981. How can I build and maintain a helping relationship with older persons? In J. E. Meyers (ed.), *Counseling older persons: Vol. 2. Basic helping skills for service providers* (pp.59-105). Alexandria, Va.: American Association for Counseling and Development.

Bratter, B., and E. Tuvman. 1980. A peer counseling program in action. In S. Sargent (ed.), *Nontraditional counseling and therapy with the aged* (pp. 131-145). New York: Springer.

Butler, R. N., and M. I. Lewis. 1982. *Aging and mental health: Positive psychosocial approaches.* St. Louis: Mosby.

Colangelo, N., and C. J. Pulvino. 1980. Some basic concerns in counseling the elderly. *Counseling and Values* 24:68-73.

Corey, G. 1985. *Theory and practice of group counseling (2nd ed.)* Pacific Grove, Cal.: Brooks/Cole.

Corey, M. S., and G. Corey. 1987. *Group counseling: Process and practice (3rd ed.).* Pacific Grove, Cal.: Brooks/Cole.

Corrigan, J. D., D. M. Dell, K. N. Lewis, K. N., and L. D. Schmidt. 1980. Counseling as a social influence process: A review [Monograph]. *Journal of Counseling Psychology* 27: 395-4411.

Dies, R. R. 1973. Group therapist self-disclosure: An evaluation by clients. *Journal of Counseling Psychology* 20:344-348.

Egan, G. 1982. *The skilled helper (2nd ed.).* Pacific Grove, Cal.: Brooks/Cole.

Ganikos, M. L. 1979. Introduction. In M. L. Ganikos (ed.), *Counseling the aged: A training syllabus for educators* (pp. vii-x). Alexandria, Va.: American Association for Counseling and Development.

Goodyear, R. K., and J. Robyak. 1981. Counseling as an interpersonal influence process: Prospective for counseling practice. *Personnel and Guidance Journal*, 60:654-657.

Haley, J. 1976. *Problem-solving therapy*. San Francisco: Jossey-Bass.

Heppner, P., and D. Dixon. 1981. A review of the interpersonal influence in counseling. *Personnel and Guidance Journal* 60:542-550.

Herr, J., and Weakland, J. 1979. *Counseling elders and their families*. New York: Springer.

Ivey, A. E., with L. Slimek-Downing, L. 1980. *Counseling and psychotherapy: Skills, theories, and practice*. Englewood Cliffs, N. J.: Prentice-Hall.

Johnson, D., and R. Matross. 1977. Interpersonal influence in psychotherapy: A social psychological review. In G. Gorman and A. Razin (eds.), *Effective psychology: A handbook of research* (pp. 395-432). New York: Pergamon Press.

Johnson, D., and H. C. Riker. 1982. Goals and roles of gerontological counselors. *American Mental Health Counselors Association Journal* 4:30-40.

Kastenbaum, R. 1968, August. *Perspectives on the developmental modification of behavior in the aged: A developmental field perspective*. Paper presented at the 76th annual convention of the American Psychological Association, San Francisco.

Kotter, J. 1979. Power, dependence, and effective management. In *Harvard Business Review: On human relations*. (pp. 359-374). New York: Harper and Row.

Lawton, M. P. 1978. Clinical geropsychology: Problems and prospects. In *Master lectures on the psychology of aging*. Washington, D. C.: American Psychological Association.

Lombana, J. H. 1976. Counseling the elderly: Remediation plus prevention. *Personnel and Guidance Journal* 55: 143-144.

McCaslin, R. 1983. *The older person as a mental health worker*. New York: Springer.

McClelland, P. J., and P. Burnham. 1979. Power is the great motivator. In *Harvard Business Review: On human relations* (pp. 341-358). New York: Harper & Row.

Meyers, J. E., and L. C. Loesch. 1981. The counseling needs of older persons. *Humanistic Educator* 20:21-35.

Minuchin, S. 1974. *Families and family therapy*. Cambridge, Mass.: Harvard University Press.

Nyburg, D. 1981. A concept of power in education. *Teachers College Record* 82:535-551.

O'Brien, C., J. Johnson, and B. Miller. 1979. Counseling the aging: Some practical considerations. *Personnel and Guidance Journal* 57:288-291.

Peters, G. 1971. Self-conceptualizations of the aged, identification, and aging. *Gerontologist* 11:69-73.

Ponzo, Z. 1978. Age prejudice of "Act your age." *Personnel and Guidance Journal* 57:140-144.

Riker, H. C. 1981. Gerontological counseling. In J. E. Meyers, P. Finnerly-Fried, and C. H. Graves (eds.), *Counseling older persons: Vol. 1. Guidelines for a team approach to training* (pp. 3-9). Alexandria, Va.: American Association for Counseling and Development.

Robison, E. A., and F. F. Robison. 1989. *Evaluation of a telephone visitor project utilizing nursing home residents.* Manuscript submitted for publication.

Smaby, M. H., T. L. Peterson, W. Tennyson, and A. Tamminen. 1988. Power is not a four letter word. *School Counselor* 36:136-145.

Strong, S. 1978. Counseling: An interpersonal influence process. *Journal of Counseling Psychology* 18:106-110.

Waters, E. B. 1984. Building on what you know: Individual and group counseling with older people. *Counseling Psychologist* 12: 52-64.

Waters, E. B., and L. M. Epstein. 1980. No person is an island: The importance of support systems in working with older people. *Counseling Psychologist* 12:52-64.

Waters, E. B., S. Reiter, B. White, and B. Dates. 1979. The role of paraprofessional peer counselors in working with older people. In M. L. Ganikos (ed.), *Counseling the aged* (pp. 229-263). Alexandria, Va.: American Association for Counseling and Development.

Waters, E. B., and A. L. Weaver. 1981. Specialized techniques to help older people. In J. E. Myers (ed.) *Counseling older persons: Vol. 2. Basic helping skills for service providers* (pp. 107-132). Alexandria, Va.: American Association for Counseling and Development.

From Journal of Mental Health Counseling *11(3):259-272.* Copyright 1989 by American Mental Health Counselors Association. Reprinted by permission of Sage Publications, Inc.

About the Authors

Daun D. Blain, M. S., is a senior certified addictions counselor with Lake-Cook Psychologists and Counseling Associates, Arlington Heights, Illinois.

Harry M. Brown, Ph.D., is a licensed clinical psychologist specializing in drug abuse treatment in Kansas City, Missouri.

Gary L. Donovan is Director of Career Planning and Placement Services at the University of Minnesota, Morris, and a licensed psychologist with Harley Clinics of Western Minnesota, Inc.

Anne L. Ganley is a psychologist with the Seattle Veterans' Administration Medical Center in Seattle, Washington, and is also in private practice.

Jerry Larke is a psychologist in private practice in Marshfield, Massachusetts, where he works with a geriatric mental health program.

Flynn O'Malley, Ph.D., is director of the Hillcrest Unit in the Children's Division of The Menninger Clinic, Topeka, Kansas.

Robert Rencken is a mental health counselor and clinical sexologist in private practice with El Dorado Psychological Associates in Tucson, Arizona. He specializes in treating sexual abuse, working with children, offenders, families, and adult survivors.

Floyd F. Robison is an assistant professor of counselor education/counseling psychology at the School of Education, Indiana University-IUPUI, specializing in gerontological counseling, group counseling, and therapeutic outcomes of counselor/client reassignments.

Marlowe H. Smaby is a professor of psychology and Research Center Director in the College of Education and Human Service Professions at the University of Minnesota, Duluth.

Gregg J. Stockey, M. S., is a certified substance abuse counselor with Lake-Cook Psychologists and Counseling Associates, Arlington Heights, Illinois.

Glenn D. Walters is the coordinator of the Drug Abuse Program at the Federal Correctional Institution in Fairton, New Jersey.

ALSO AVAILABLE . . .

Especially for the counselor

Counseling the Involuntary and Resistant Client
George A. Harris, Ph.D., David Watkins, Ph.D.

Practical advice for counselors, officers, medical teams, and others working with clients who don't want to be helped. Reviews the causes and the types of resistant behavior and offers useful techniques for working with these clients. *(1987, 112 pages, 0-942974-87-5, #350)*

The Elements of Short-term Group Counseling
Elllis S. Grayson

A basic resource manual for front-line personnel, this primer provides a concise, straightforward approach to using short-term group counseling in institutional and community settings. Details how to introduce, plan, and carry out a successful group counseling program. *(2nd edition, 1989, 106 pages, 0-929310-10-1, #138)*

Correctional Counseling
David Lester and Michael Braswell

A valuable text on offender counseling, including keys to understanding criminal behavior, diagnosis, and classification. A comprehensive look at the variety of therapies available. Discussion questions at the end of each chapter. *(1987, 238 pages, 0-87084-371-0, #359)*

Call 1-800-825-2665 to order!

The American Correctional Association   8025 Laurel Lakes Court   Laurel, Maryland 20707-5075